Hidden Techniques of Karate

A martial arts video course book.

Previously Published as 'Chiang Nan'

Al Case

QUALITY PRESS

For complete information go to: MonsterMartialArts.com

TABLE OF CONTENTS

COMPLETE LIST OF BOOKS AND VIDEOS BY AL CASE

MARTIAL ARTS
How to Create Kenpo 1
How to Create Kenpo 2
How to Create Kenpo 3
Pan Gai Noon Karate/Kung Fu
Kang Duk Won Korean Karate
Kwon Bup American Karate
Outlaw Karate
Buddha Crane Karate
Karate to Shaolin to Pa Kua Chang
Matrixing Tong Bei
Fixing MCMAP 1
Fixing MCMAP 2
Bruce Lee vs Classical Martial Arts
Shaolin Butterfly
Butterfly Pa Kua Chang
The Hardest Punch in the World
How to be a Master Instructor
Matrix Karate: White Belt
Matrix Karate: Green Belt
Matrix Karate: Brown Belt
Matrix Karate: Black Belt
Matrix Karate: Master
Binary Matrixing
How to Matrix the Martial Arts
The Master Text
How to Matrix Kick Boxing
Monkey Boxing Forms
Matrixing Chi

Yoga
Yogata: The Yoga Kata
Black Belt Yoga

Children
Universal Glue
Return of the Dragon

Miscellaneous
Truth About Algebra
Pig Latin
Blood and Ink (How to Write)

NOVELS
Spreadwing
Grave Business
The North Mansion
The Haunting of House
Machina
Monkeyland
The Bomber's Story 1 & 2
The Lone Star Revolt
Yancy
Return to Monkeyland
Small in the Saddle
When the Cold Wind Blows
Path of the Snake
Path of the Wizard
Path of the Dragon
Twisted Gods
Hero
Assassin
Avatar
Falling Skies
Pack
Fugue
The Mortal Coil
Ethereal Bodyguard
The Day They Bombed LA
Day the President Killed the US
Light of the Insane Yogi's Eyeballs
How to Kill
Curse of the Gods
Lobo Love
Lobo University
The Naked Witch
15th Chapter
Transformation of George Cogswell
Little Girls

SPECIAL NOTE

At the beginning of some chapters you will find links to videos showing the forms.

If these links do not work, then retain your receipt for the book(s) and email me for new links.

This is likely to happen as links can corrode over time, websites can be taken down, replaced, and so on.

Aganzul@gmail.com.

introduction

One time I decided to write a series of novels. I wanted to be commercial, so I decided to write four novels, picking a different crime for each one. I wrote and I wrote and I wrote, and a funny thing happened. Midway through the third novel I sat back, blinked, and realized that I was working on one novel.

I thought it was four! But, in truth, it would have made four, lousy, piss ant short novels.

But, if I rearranged the chapters, I had one, massive, killer of a novel.

So I did it, and the name of the novel is 'The Bomber's Story.'

Furthermore, I was shocked to find out that The Bomber's Story was part of a five book series. So I wrote the other three books (I had already written one and didn't know it), and had a massive series mixing sci fi, mystery, alien technology, all sorts of things.

So what does this have to do with Martial Arts?

This book is like that novel.

I started it, people sent me emails out of the blue, I came across research by other people, I made discoveries, and I found that I had a book that had three different approaches.

So…what do I call it?

Originally, I was going to call it 'Translating Karate into Tai Chi.' I reworked forms, sorted through concepts, and I was madly typing and then things happened.

Then I was going to call it 'Chiang Nan: The Lost Form.' I had been doing the five karate forms as one form for decades, I had reworked them into what I felt was a true representation of the way I thought the original form (from which they had been drawn) from a hundred years ago, and… something happened.

Then I was thinking of calling it 'The Lost Bunkai Techniques of Karate: Deliberately Hidden by Ancient Masters.'

And…something happened.

So, all these things happening, the different story lines coming together into one whomper stomper, the book lives up to all the titles.

I think I will issue several versions, all the same except for the titles.

Heck, that's just marketing, and hopefully I will be able to reach people with one title who might not feel the appeal of another title.

So, be warned. Don't buy all the versions, just find the one that has the title you like the best.

And, with that said, let me give a whomper stomper of a martial arts manual.

It will translate karate into Tai Chi.

It will offer the best visualization I have of the original form from which all karate grew.

It will give you the original bunkai (techniques) of karate. Techniques that were deliberately hidden by the old Masters, and which were thought to be lost.

And, it will give you a lot more.

Because the original form was a seed, and that seed has flowered. But each of you are a seed, and the flowering will continue unimaginable.

In short, creation is the breakdown and synthesis of the old into the new.

That act of synthesis has certainly been done here, and you will continue it.

Have a great work out!

Al Case

Chapter One
Karate/Tai Chi Concepts

Most martial artists are influenced by this art or that art.

They study one art for a while, it is their base art, their favorite art, but each art they come across has something to add.

On one hand, this is good, any time you learn something it is good.

On the other hand, this has created a huge mess, a confusion of concepts, a breeding of styles and philosophies that don't actually mesh.

With matrixing I address the huge and terrible inbreeding of martial arts. I align the styles with concepts, show how to break arts into their pure nature, and how to view the martial arts as a single whole.

And then a person is able to mesh concepts without danger.

In this book I am translating one art into another: karate into Tai Chi.

And, of course, there will be much reverse engineering here; a person will see a potential translation of Tai Chi to Karate.

All this will be possible because there is a good historical evolution here, one that can be observed and gleaned with a fair amount of clarity.

In translating one must take into account not just the art, but the evolutions of the art, the cultural lineages, what the original concepts were.

Thus, to translate, we must first look at two items, the concepts of Karate, and the concepts of Tai Chi.

By understanding them apart from one another we will be able to borrow and transfigure. We will be able to change one into the other.

If you try to hold to one concept pure the translation won't work.

If you expect karate to look like Tai Chi, it won't. And Tai chi won't look like Karate.

But there will be concepts that will shift and realign; there will be ways to make this thing work. As bastards go, it should work.

KARATE CONCEPTS

Karate concepts can be summed up by something I call 'Basic-basics.' Interestingly, these concepts are shared by all arts.
The differences are in shadings of force versus flow.
The first karate basic-basic is:

Breathing

Breath to the tan tien. The Tan Tien translates as 'The One Point.' It is located a couple of inches below the navel. It is the energy generator for the body.

You always breath as if to the Tan Tien.

Air can't reach the tan tien, but air can be felt down to the diaphragm, and sensation of air becomes the sensation of energy, an actual wave of feeling, down to the tan tien.

If you stand relaxed, with feet shoulder width apart and the arms out to the sides, and breath to the tan tien, you should feel a tingling in your finger tips.

Through the martial arts, specifically through the forms and techniques, you can learn to channel this energy.

Breath in when the body contracts, breath out when it expands.

Breath out when you block or strike, or when you get struck.

Breath as if to the body part being used, let the sensation of energy build, create shield and spear.

Relaxing

Energy flows best through that which is relaxed.

If you lock your fist, energy will lock in that fist. This is good for striking and blocking.

Learn to relax always.

Use breathing to relax.

Grounding

Grounding is to sink the weight, to use gravity. This must be done in conjunction with a study of stances.

When the body feels weight the tan tien works, it creates energy that is usable by the person, it can be channeled to parts of the body.

If you stand high in a stance the body works a little, and little energy is created.

If you stand low in a stance the body works hard, and lots of energy is created.

Thus, when one practices low stances he is building a reservoir of energy.

There is a formula for this:

Weight = Work = Energy

In the study of karate, or other arts, one learns how to channel down one leg or another, and this is specific to stances.

If one breathes properly, and learns to relax in deep stances, the energy builds quicker and is even more usable. Energy, after all, flows easier through that which is relaxed.

This seeming contradiction, the hard work of stances made effortless, is the secret of chi power in the martial arts.

Body Alignment

To build chi power through the afore mentioned method is only half the game. One must learn to use that energy. Thus, we have the study of body alignment.

The static method of learning to use energy is to merely look at the martial arts postures, press on the postures, and learn to guide the energy into the ground.

This is called body testing.

Stand in, for instance, a back stance, and hold a middle block.

If the stance and block are correct a person can press on them and they won't give way.

You have to press in the correct manner, which means you need to understand body alignment and how it works.

The person being pressed upon must focus on breathing, and relaxing, and learn how to feel the sensation of energy passing through the body.

Most important, he must learn how to make his resistance effortless. He must reduce muscular resistance and learn how to rely on the channeling of energy.

Coordinated Body Motion

Coordinated Body Motion, or CBM, is learning to move all parts of the body in conjunction.

The feet and the hands start motion at the same time, and they stop at the same time.

Further, you must calibrate the distances body parts are being moved and move them appropriate in distance.

If a hand moves in a circle that is six feet in circumference, and the feet move only one foot in a line, and the time taken for the move is ten seconds, then the hands must move six feet per ten seconds and the feet must move one foot per second.

You must learn how to do this for ALL movements in a form.

Learning to move like this is sometimes called 'using the body as one unit.'

My description, however, is much more scientific, and easier to apply to all movements, regardless of the level of the practitioner, the difficulty of the form, and so on.

TYING IT ALL TOGETHER

This concept of CBM must be utilized not just in the gross motions of the body, but in the installation of basic-basics to the body.

Breathing must be CBMed. Sinking must be CBMed. Everything you do, in all of life, must be CBMed.

To CBM will make the body one unit, which leads to harmony in motion, which leads to the manufacture and evolution and growth of intention.

It is intention which ties everything together.

It is not muscle, it is not the ligament which moves the muscle, it is not the nerve impulse which tells the ligament to move the muscle, it is not the spark in the brain that tells the nerves to tell the ligaments to move the muscle.

It is he who moves the muscle.

It is the human being, the spirit, the 'I am,' which causes the spark to communicate through the nerve to tighten the ligament and muscle.

But this will all become clear, should you simply follow the directions listed in this chapter through a sincere course of study in the martial arts.

TAI CHI CHUAN CONCEPTS

Tai Chi Chuan is not so simple as karate, on the surface.

Yet, scratch, and you will find a high and polished degree of simplicity.

The problem is that Tai Chi Chuan, while being highly evolved, has lived through the influences of literally thousands of evolutions of artistic concepts.

So, how do we find the simple truth of that long and profound art?

Basic-Basics

First, breathing, relaxing and grounding are the same as in Karate.

This is incredibly obvious if one simply does the form.

And body alignment and CBM are the same.

So what is the difference?

Karate is considered, rightly or wrongly, a 'linear' art. It explodes, and manifests in straight line strategies.

TCC, on the other hand, absorbs.

It goes the other way.

Karate charges, TCC retreats.

Karate is force, TCC is flow.

This is a broad simplicity, but true enough to be considered true for these pages, and the work we do herein.

Force versus Flow

Here is the interesting result to this difference of force versus flow.

When one flows one becomings 'emptier' than if one explodes.

Explosion is a manifestation of force from the inception. Explosion is indiscriminate, runs into 'objects,' and creates more force.

Tai Chi Chuan, on the other hand, goes with whatever flow there is, becoming even, for lack of a better 'word,' 'flowier.'

Thus, Tai Chi reveals one of the profound secrets of the universe, which secret elevates it above other martial arts: true power is in emptiness.

More chi flows, energy is much more responsive, the intention of the individual grows exponentially in relation to other arts.

And, I would be remiss, at this point, if I did not mention the Force/ Flow Formula.

If the force is greater flow it,
if the flow is greater force it.

This is a tremendous stratagem which evolves directly from the yin yang concept, which is the supreme description of this universe, and which states:

For something to be true,
the opposite must also be true.

Through this formula the martial arts - ALL the martial arts — are discoverable.

Indeed, ALL of the universe is discoverable.

The Universe and Time

The universe is nothing but objects moving through space.

We conquer the universe through the illusions of measurement; physics. I say illusion for physics, mathematics, all manner of description, is made up by us so as to share concepts.

The heart of physics is measurement of objects through space.

Thus, we enter the illusion of distance, and the description of distance, which is time.

Time is distance, and distance is time; this is the truth of physics.

Now, the truth of the martial arts is that if you control distance you control the fight.

And, to control distance one will control time.

In short, every person has his own sense of time, unique and separate from the time of the universe.

One thing that people don't understand, is that one can, through a sincere practice of the martial arts, learn to control his own personal time to the extend that it controls the time of another person.

And, in the extreme, controls the time of the universe.

Which brings us to Tai Chi Chuan, and the supreme method of learning to control time.

Tai Chi Chuan and Time

First, make sure your basic-basics are working.

Breath, relax, ground, align your body, CBM.

And when you move you must move like the hands of a clock.

Tick, tick, tick, remorseless. Your hands circling like a sweep hand, never slowing, never speeding.

And your feet moving in appropriate CBM manner.

In the beginning the circuit of the clock does not happen in sixty seconds; your hands might describe a circle in ten seconds.

Or eight or twelve, whatever works for you to keep the form interesting.

You control your limbs so there is no shake or quiver, especially in the balance upon the stance.

The hands circle, and you watch them, and in the watching a unique realization occurs.

It is you that are watching, and watching becomes extremely pleasurable.

Most people travel through this universe without watching, being victims of the universe, adjusting their time to whatever time the universe imposes upon them, actually thinking they are part of the universe.

The Tai Chi Chuanist, through the manipulation of his own body, through the discipline of his own mind, controls his time, and ultimately learns to impose his sense of time upon the opponent, and then the universe itself.

A Couple of Other Concepts

In karate you will get this sense of time, but it will take longer.

And, in Karate, there are other concepts that you will enjoy which are not as available, at least not in the short term, in Tai Chi Chuan.

One art is not superior to the other, you see; they both offer concepts separate, but which can be joined and transferred depending upon the understanding and ability of the student.

For instance:

Karate is Explosive strength.

Tai Chi is Suspended strength.

In karate one uses muscles, and eventually finds chi.

In Tai Chi one uses chi directly.

In karate one summons power through focus, which is described by the term 'loose-tight.' One is loose, focuses his strength (muscles) by becoming tight, then goes back to loose.

In Tai Chi one is loose, and attempts to remain loose. There is no tight.

Though, to be sure, evolution in the case of both will lead to the focus of chi power in strike, block, shielding the body, and so on.

The Translation

When doing the karate form, or Chiang Nan, or Channan, you use breathing, relaxing and grounding.

You use alignment and CBM.

You move slowly, watching the hands make their circuit, and realize the feeling of one motion guiding the whole form. You follow the hand without break, realize there is no break, and reach the end of the form.

The techniques will have a karate flavor to them, but they will also elongate over what you may have experienced in Karate techniques before.

This is an interesting point, an old saying: a technique never ends with a block.

But if you look at the forms they are filled with blocks that seem to end the action. This is because the old masters on Okinawa gave the beginning of the technique, not the whole technique. They made pact not to show the true art, so they would show half a motion, and only the favored student would receive instruction revealing the missing half.

So you will find, if not in the forms, in the applications, the completion of motion, the last half of ten uniques that have been left out.

Mind you, it is my reverse engineering, my experience in many arts, my matrixing technology, but I am sure many people will agree with what I have done.

Or, at least, be driven to think about what I have done and come to their own conclusions.

There will be a little absorption, but this will be most in guiding attacks through the 'slap/grab' concept, which I feel is at the heart of the art.

There will be circles, but they will not be large and slow.

There will be subtle shifts of weight and small manipulations that guide the whole of a technique.

Most of all, there will be awareness.

Conclusion

So, you have the summation, move slow, create circles, look for the completion of a action…don't stop on a block.

But what is karate?

What is Tai Chi?

What are the martial arts?

They are systems of self-defense…but they are more.

The martial arts are a discipline that enhance physical survival.

But, more, they are a discipline which finds the source of the human being (the spirit, the 'I am) and guide it to more awareness.

Without awareness you are an animal. Slugging and bashing and scrabbling for survival.

But survival of what?

Not the body, for that dies.

For the spirit.

The martial arts build awareness, and that awareness elevates one from the mud and into higher realms.

But the key is awareness.

Don't just blast.

Don't just fight.

Find awareness, instill awareness in your movements.

Find the glow that awareness brings, and instill it into your life, every aspect of your life.

Good journey.

Chapter Two
Chi Concepts

Below are the videos introducing Tai Chi concepts.

brush knee and app 1 ~ https://youtu.be/2rJPLnOIaco	7:29
brush knee app 1 ~ https://youtu.be/5yy3FcFJlzw	5:42
Slant Flying and apps ~ https://youtu.be/PH-T49WX3Sg	17:58
brush knee ~ https://youtu.be/Mo72caPdh2U	5:41
slant flying ~ https://youtu.be/0n2JLHv5M5g	7:02
Fair Lady ~ https://youtu.be/3Z-2xq4Xh8I	5:51
	49:43

Beyond the concepts specific to Karate, and to Tai Chi Chuan, there is a third set of concepts we should go into. These are the concepts of generating and developing chi.

Chi is energy, and there are many types of it.

Gross chi would be the energy created by fire, hydraulics, etc.

Fine chi would be that chi generated and guided through 'mental power.'

I say mental power, but actually it is spirit that generates and guides chi. It is intention, which is the will to do something, the desire to do something.

The martial arts are probably the best way to generate and develop chi on this planet. They do this through discipline, ridding oneself of distractions, and building one's will power, or spirit.

The following steps are the steps I use top generate and guide chi power. They work through any martial art, but specifically through those that have forms.

It is best if the forms are matrixed, and that every move is thoroughly understood as an application.

The best way of understanding chi, of actually feeling it, is to relate it to other forms of energy.

For instance, fire burns…and the tan tien 'burns.'

Water flows and swirls, and you can feel the sensation of chi flowing and swirling like water on the inside.

Moving and thrusting your hands through air gives a distinct sensation.

Throwing chi feels like throwing a baseball. Not a distinct sensation, like water or air, but a sensation of generating motion and letting go of a ball.

Always search for an 'analogy' for your motion.

Here are the twelve things I do.

1
Holding the Bowl

This is a very old method of creating chi. It establishes certain factors that must be adhered to through all methods for generating chi.

These factors include such things as sinking the weight (grounding), relaxing, breathing, feeling the sensation (like very gentle electricity) as you gently will awareness around the macrocosmic orbit. (The macrocosmic orbit is the centerline of the body, running down the front and up the back.)

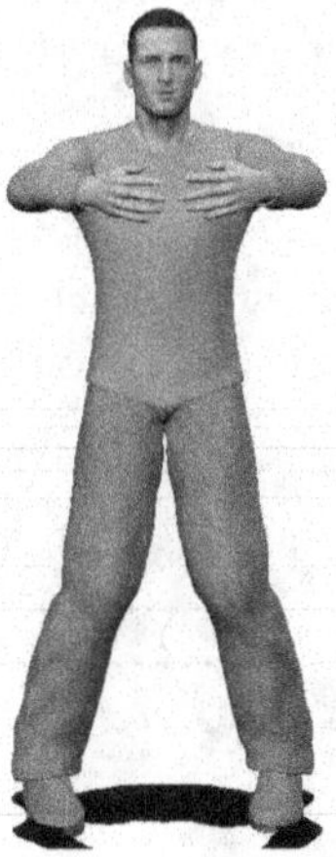

Feel chi circle the arms. Feel the chi bridge the gap between the fingers (one inch). Imagine your arms as having a metal hoop in them, a hoop that cannot be bent or pulled apart.

I once decided to adapt this drill to Wing Chun. The specific point I was pursuing was to have EXACTLY equal amounts of energy in both arms; to balance, perfectly, the right and the left, and this while doing Sticky Hands.

I adjusted the forces in both arms till I thought i had it, then I took a deep breath, exhaled, and focused on the the space between the fingers.

I instantly found myself totally apart from my body. I was a dot of awareness. I was immortal and all powerful.

I was also terrified. I didn't know what to do.

My partner didn't know what was happening; he felt like a huge hand had reached down and gripped his whole body; he was firmly in the grasp of my spirit.

I finally managed to break the situation by striking my opponent. He was thrust across the room, his whole body, and smacked against the wall like a fly hitting a windshield.

2
Slosh the Tub

I call it 'sloshing the tub' for the simple reason that I don't know what else describes it so perfectly.

I stand in a tai chi stance and move back and forth. I can feel energy sloshing back and forth inside my body, and it feels like water in a bathtub.

To do this you must be connected to the ground, and preferably in stance.

The first step is simply to move left to right, just sway, deepening the stance gradually.

Make sue you synchronize your breathing with the motion. In as you push off a leg, out as you sink the weight on a leg.

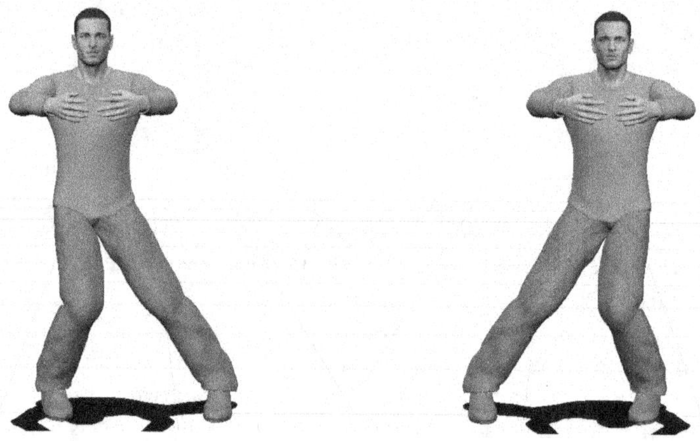

I am holding the bowl in the above images, but you don't have to. In fact, it is sometimes better if you start out just letting your arms hang, then look for arm positioning later on, when the chi is really flowing and perceptible.

I also, sometimes, imagine a tennis ball inside a leg.

Up and down the legs in time with the breathing.

3
Swirl the Chi

Hold a glass half filled with water and swirl the water. This should be what happens when you do the following drill.

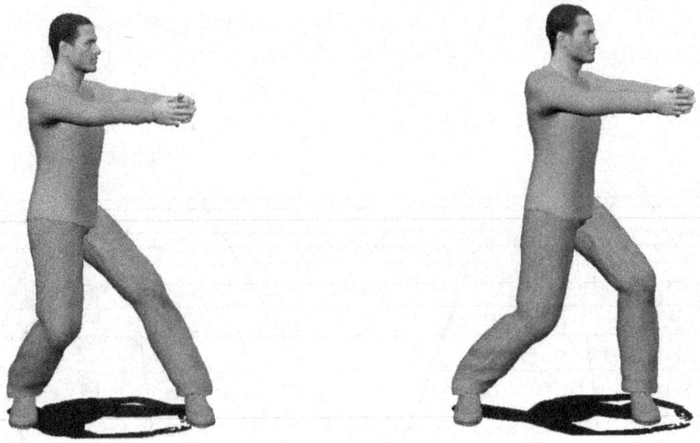

Turn and sink into a back stance. Push with back leg into front stance.

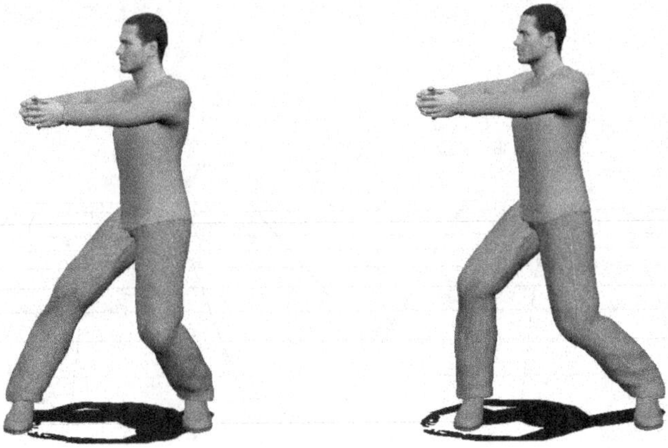

Turn the hips and sink into back stance. Push with the back leg into a front stance.

Focus on sloshing, then swirling.

Let the chi slosh back and forth, then feel it swirling inside the body.

Let the arms hang at first, then go explore arm positioning.

Search for the slosh in every change of body positioning. Don't be afraid to adapt forms to better find 'swirling.'

Make sure you go back and explore the original position later on, after a few months, to make sure you haven't missed something, have strong (perceiving enough) to find the chi in the original positions, and so on.

Eventually you should be able to feel (diurect) the chi into body parts.

You can put chi into organs just by being aware of your organs.

You can, and this is especially useful for combat, put chi into the arms in the various arm positions. This leads to a finer understanding off Swirling.

Tubing

To apply this concept of moving chi in the body to moving chi into a punch or block, or even kick, simply imagine the arm as a two inch PVC pipe half filled with sand.

Thrust the tube suddenly, mimicking the motion of an arm in strike, and feel the sand rush down the tube and gather in the end (focus).

You can also swirl the tube, then stop the tube motion suddenly (focus), and feel the sand push against the side of the tube.

It is quite useful to do this exercise with a real tube filled with sand, or perhaps water.

4
Duplicating the Hands

The energy in the tan tien mimics the motions of the hands.

That is, you turn the hands down, and the chi rushes down the legs.

You point, and the chi rushes in the direction you are pointing.

This can be quite useful when body testing a person, and especially to verify that you have reached a certain point in your chi building exercises.

For instance, you push on somebody and they withstand the push. You then point in a direction, and they become unbalanced if you are pushing in the direction you are pointing, or if you just point upwards (takes their mind off grounding). Eventually you point inside your mind, and they become unbalanced. I do caution you not to do this too often as it tends to invalidate student's and can even undermine their efforts.

I love to hold an imaginary softball and go through the earlier exercises. I roll the ball in my hands as I slosh and swirl. After doing this for a couple of years I was able to imagine myself as in a giant ball of energy. The small ball in my hands had been mimicked by my tan tien, and my had grown sufficient to be perceived as a giant ball.

Talk about fighting in 3D.

It's fun to play dragon ball and know the reality of it.

5
Watching the Finger

I began doing this in Pa Kua, adapted it to Tai Chi, and then to other arts. It is very reminiscent of the 'iron thread' movement in Shaolin.

First, I stand in an hourglass stance and watch my finger, then I circle the finger in front of me.

Eventually I begin moving it through the various drills. I slosh and I swirl.

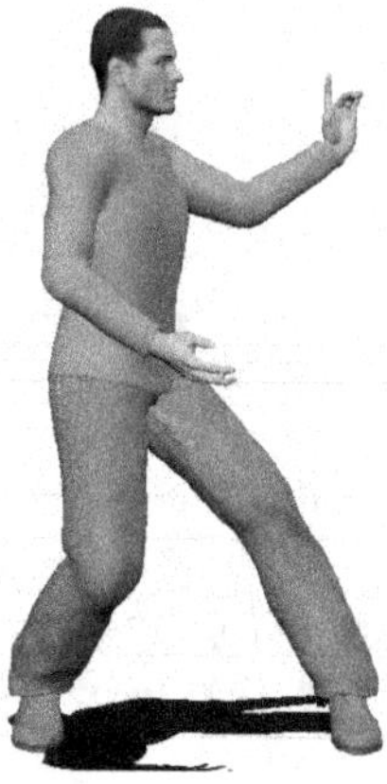

Eventually I go through my form, watching my finger instead of blocking and striking, merely putting my finger into reasonable assumption of position. I slosh and I swirl, and I become aware of the energy moving into my finger.

Eventually I began drawing 'sparkler-like' circles in the air.

I used to think that only I could see these circles, then one day a student became very excited, saying he could see the cocoon swirling around me.

6
Come from the Center

Coming from the center is simply to base all movement from the tan tien.

On the physical side, this means to align the body parts from the tan tien.

If you align your body correctly the chi will flow.

I would give you a picture here, but that would be silly. This is the point of whole arts, and specifically of matrixing.

Align the body in static posture so that one can press on the body and the energy goes through the body, the tan tien, and down the legs and into the ground.

Once the body is correctly aligned, apply the concept to motion by studying CBM (Coordinated body Motion).

CBM is when all body parts start motion at the same time, and end at the same time.

CBM includes the dropping of weight, rotating hips, and thrusting of body. These three points, gravity, rotation and thrust, when properly CBMed give a LARGE boost to your chi.

I was aware of all the drills I am giving you here, but my real knowledge came from not the drills, rather the fact of CBMing every motion I did.

I reverse engineered to find the drills, and was shocked by how much i had been missing, and how my progress would have been easier.

7
Circling

To move the hands in set circles while you slosh.

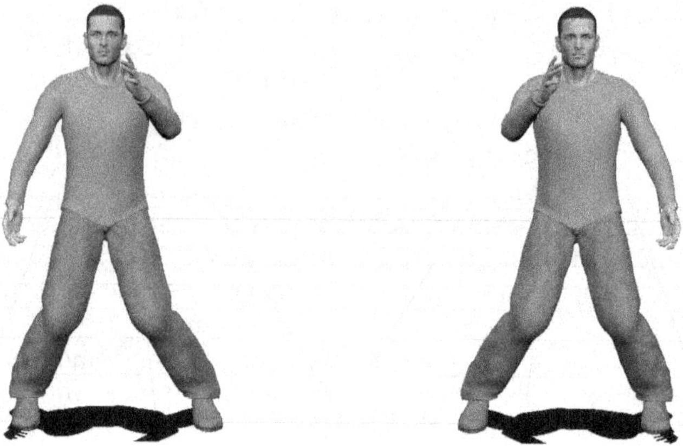

Make circles with the hands.
Right in, then left in, then right in.
Feel the weight moving back and forth inside your body.
You can adapt this drill by reversing the circles, have the circles oppose, and so on.
The main thing is to relax, let go of rigidity, and feel the chi moving about you.
This is a great drill for opening a class.

8
Slap Grab with Triangular step

The slap grab is circling with the hands (opposing circles). You can feel it back and forth in the legs, no matter what stances you choose.

The most practical stance for this drill, however, is to do a triangle step as you do it.

Slap with the feet in the natural (hourglass) stance, then execute a grab as you move one foot forward.

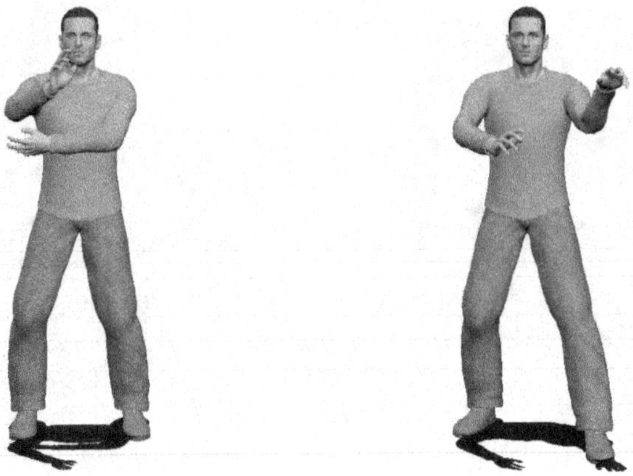

Relax the hands, feel pressure inside them, the pressure will translate to weight, and your hands will become very heavy when striking.

9
Low High (low out)

Stand in a horse stance. Twist to one side with a reverse low block. Return to the horse with a high block.

In the images below I have adapted the drill to an outward middle block.

We used to do a simple 'hip slam' (right front stance pivot to left front stance, back and forth) with a punch to the front in the Kang Duk Won. I was surprised to find out how enjoyable it was to do this drill tai chi style, and how effective. I was able to channel awareness to a much greater extent.

You should explore the moves of the form for opportunities to do this drill (with sloshing and swirling and tubing).

10
Grab and Punch

This is one of the moves from Bot Sai, or Chiang Nan 6. It reinforces the idea of searching through the form for moves from the forms you can use for chi drills.

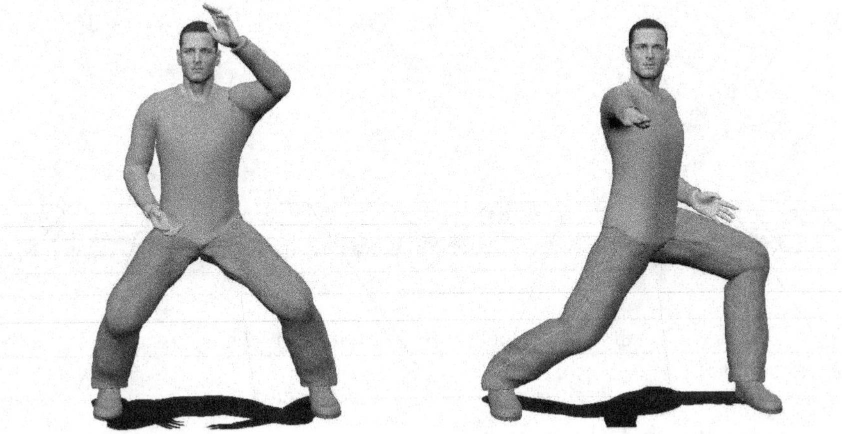

Do a slow high block in a horse stance, continue the motion of the high block to twist into a front stance and extend the spear hand.

Repeat on the other side.

You should feel sloshing, you should feel your arm as if it is moving through water. You should feel as if tunneling through air as you thrust the spear hand. You should be 'screwing' your body into the ground. You should be relaxing.

11
Low Mid Strike

This is a repeat of drill nine, or maybe a put together of nine and ten.

Do a slow reverse low block, translate into a middle outward, execute a spear hand.

This should be done slowly, slashing, swirling and tubing.

Relax, breath, feel the ground.

Draw circles in the air.

Ignore the world and become your own universe.

12
Silk Reeling

The Chinese have a term, 'silk reeling,' that describes these chi drills, especially when you explore the moves from a form, and that is what this drill is, explore the forms, each move, see if you can make circles, smooth transitions, adapt as you need.

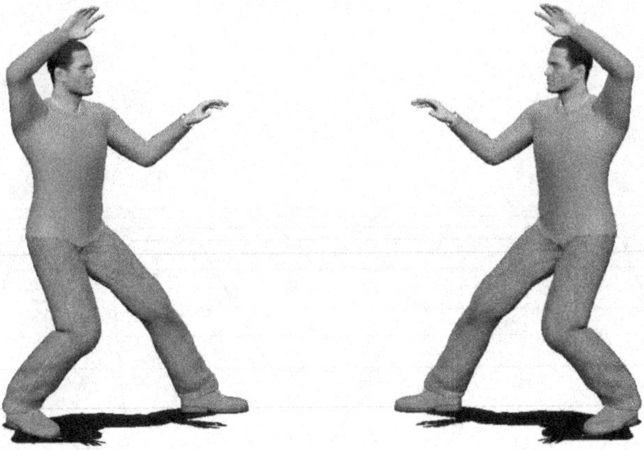

Here's the move from Chiang Nan 4. It is easy to see how you can do this and do this and do this, slashing and swirling, sinking and drawing circles, generating endless chi from the tan tien and making it real in this universe.

Taking the energy of your own personal universe and drawing upon this universe with it.

Find the circle between the second move and the third.

Move through the form, finding the circles, making them circle into each other.

When you can do the form as one long circle then you have found the truth of translating Karate into Tai Chi Chuan.

Chapter Three
Chiang Nan One

Below are the videos for form One.

channan 1 ~ https://youtu.be/ayndeGUbUQI	2:36
channan 1 side ~ https://youtu.be/1Rsx8ChuyDI	2:14
channan 1 explained ~ https://youtu.be/cLU2hwv5Y0M	7:36
channan 1 app 1 ~ https://youtu.be/mBYGz4jvHgY	4:07
channan 1 app 2 ~ https://youtu.be/ORI5NNLXm70	5:45
channan 1 app 3 ~ https://youtu.be/J-f3L0vvui8	3:05
channan 1 app 4 ~ https://youtu.be/wWh3oi1IGEQ	4:31
channan 1 app 5 ~ https://youtu.be/DhweBN04u_Q	3:28
channan 1 app 6 ~ https://youtu.be/XWcSTDnt5tc	5:58
channan 1 app 7 ~ https://youtu.be/narnQ3a55Go	5:55
	32:09

Chiang Nan One

Pinan One was once Pinan Two. And Two was Pinan One. They were switched because it was a better order to teach them in.

And, the forms were changed. Changed much.

That forms change is obvious and cannot be argued against.

Styles have different versions. Name is same, moves are different.

Why were they changed?

People evolving through the martial arts.

Changing times and customs and dress and so on demand a change of techniques.

Because of secret pacts.

What? Secret pacts? You mean somebody agreed to hide Karate? To withhold it from their own students?

You betcha.

In the book 'Hidden Karate: The True Bunkai for the Heian Katas and Naihanchi,' written by Gennosuke Higaki (pen name), on page 65, the author discusses the fact that there was a secret pact made by the Okinawan Karate masters to hide the real Karate.

To not teach the real kata (forms).

To hide the real Bunkai (techniques).

This for the simple reason of elitism. Keeping the art true for Okinawa only, and selling inferior goods to other countries and cultures.

To be honest, I knew something like this had to have happened. Through the application of Matrixing Technology, which is a logic and science of the martial arts, I could see vast, missing pieces in the lists of techniques. I could see illogics in the forms.

And, of course, there was a huge discrepancy between forms, and fighting. Simply, one could not use the forms in freestyle.

Which brought many to the obvious question: why bother with the forms?

Which had the result of people putting aside karate, altering it for fighting and tournament (without the knowledge of how karate actually worked), and a general degradation of art which has, to be honest, virtually destroyed Karate.

In addition, I had the great fortune to be taught a karate which was true. That is, there were only five links between myself and the original founders of Karate, and this lineage paralleled the Japanese lineage, but was immune to the alterations and withholdings of art done to other styles of Karate.

One interesting point, when I was a brown belt one of the students asked the instructor (Ron Maletti), who was a third black at the time, why we practiced the forms when they couldn't be used in fighting.

Ron's response was to have the class name a form, then freestyle with students using only techniques from the named form.

A number of students, myself included, were struck dumb, and received serious education, at this display of mastery.

In the end, Ron merely said: 'Don't be impatient. Study the forms. That's where the secrets lie.'

Which, some 40 years later, told me that the forms had been altered.

But the fact that a 3rd black instructor could use the forms in combat indicated that the forms hadn't been changed that much, and that we (including myself) still had the true karate.

At any rate, here are those original forms, starting with the first form, Heian One.

Or, by the previous name, Pinan One.

Or, by the original name, Chiang Nan One.

But I have altered them, in this book, in the aim of researching where they came from.

After the form you will find techniques. Techniques that have been practiced and researched by myself over the years and do give me cause to know them as original Bunkai.

Or have been the result of Matrixing, and are designed to fill the spaces left by Masters who should have known better.

You will find pressure points, throws, strikes, original concepts regarding what the art is and how it developed and what it should be.

But you have to be patient, and willing to go beyond the instructions, as thorough as they are here, on your own.

The point to be remembered here is that self defense techniques, taken from the forms, define the forms, give reality to the forms, and teach the mechanics and physics necessary to understand and master the form.

Enjoy.

A NOTE:

If you are confused by the purpose of the move, the clarification will likely be in the Promised Fights (applications) at the end of the form.

The forms should be done slowly, Tai Chi style, unless otherwise noted. Tai Chi allows awareness to enter the form. Without awareness there is no art.

Hands and feet should start motion at the same time, and end motion at the same time. This is called CBM (Coordinated Body Motion)

Seek circularity in motion. If a motion has a back and forth motion the muscles have to act twice. If a motion is circular the muscles only act once.

Breath in when the body contracts, breath out when it expands.

Breath out when you get struck. When struck breath as if breathing into the body part being struck. This is a matter of channeling awareness, which awareness will become chi power.

The form is a template; adjust the template to fit incoming forces and flows. Do not overly change the form, learn to adapt it.

Some of these moves may appear strange, unorthodox. Be patient. You will find, when you do the applications, that we are defining better ways of motion, and constructing the body according to physics pertinent to combat.

Always strive for reality in your training.

CHIANG NAN ONE

Stand squarely in the room (natural stance). This means to stand without leaning in any direction, so that you can move without having to 'pre-move.'

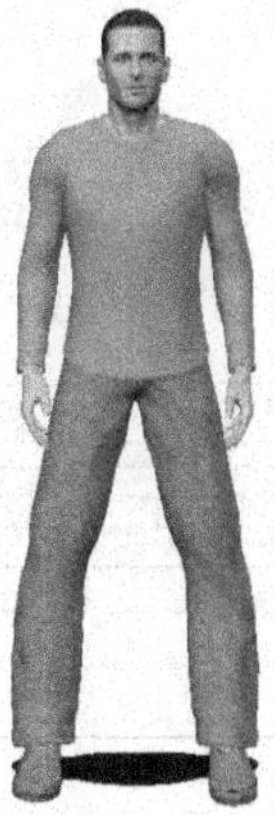

Step back with the left foot as you circle the right hand preparatory to a low block.

This will shift the weight slightly to the right leg, which will set up the push into the low block.

Low Block ~ Step forward with the left foot into a front stance as you execute a left low block.

Step back with the left foot. The left hand circles outward as if catching/guiding an incoming punch.

The footwork of this and the next image describe the 'Switch Step.' With the Switch Step one foot goes half the distance back to the rear foot, then the rear foot goes forward a complete step.

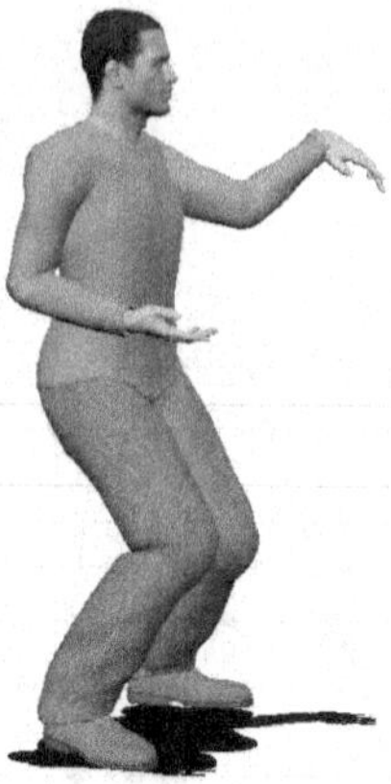

Step forward with the right foot. The left arm completes the circle back to the chamber position, the right fist executes a lunging punch.

Step forward with the left foot, halfway to the right foot, then pivot 180 degrees and step forward with the right foot as you execute a left low block.

This is a Switch Step with a turn.

The right hand does not chamber or pause in this move, it goes from the punch to the low block in one smooth move, and in perfect time with the feet.

A NOTE:

One should always use the body as one unit. This is called CBM, or Coordinated Body Motion. The hands and feet start at the same time, they stop at the same time. Every part of the body contributes, appropriate to their construction, mass, and so forth, to the intention of the move.

One move has but one intention.

Never split your intention.

Retract the right foot slightly into a back stance as you roll the left fist. The hips should square in this move.

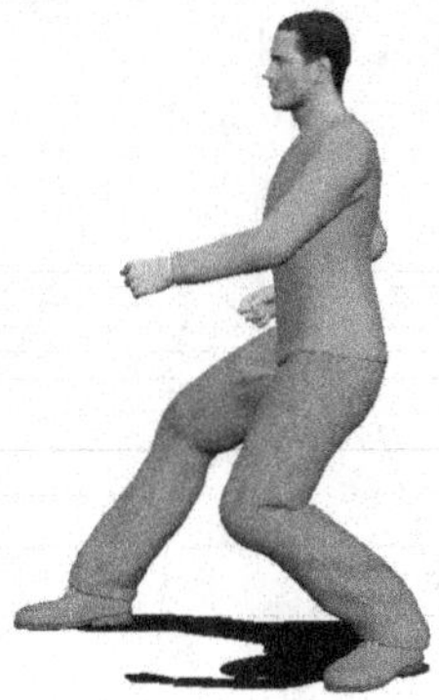

Roll the right fist. Make sure you turn the hips.

These two punches should be done like a blink.

Step forward with the left foot as you execute a right arm circle and a left lunging punch.

The Switch Step is not needed here as the back stance has already created the proper set up for the Lunging Punch; the back leg is bent and 'springable.'

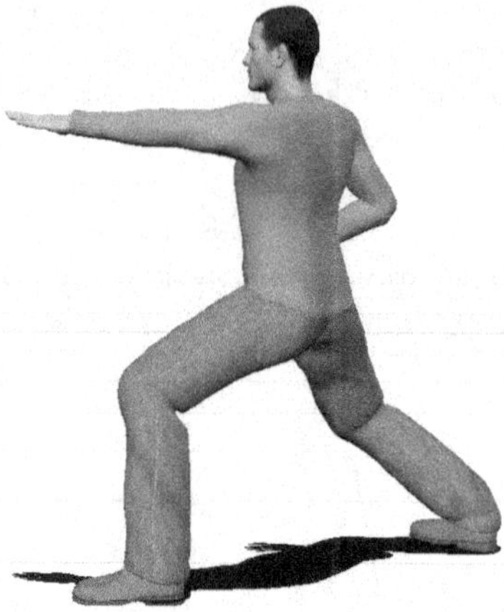

Bring the left foot back and pivot 90 degrees to the left into a cat stance. Guard the face with the right palm and prepare the right hand for a low block.

Step forward with the left foot into a front stance as you execute a left low block.

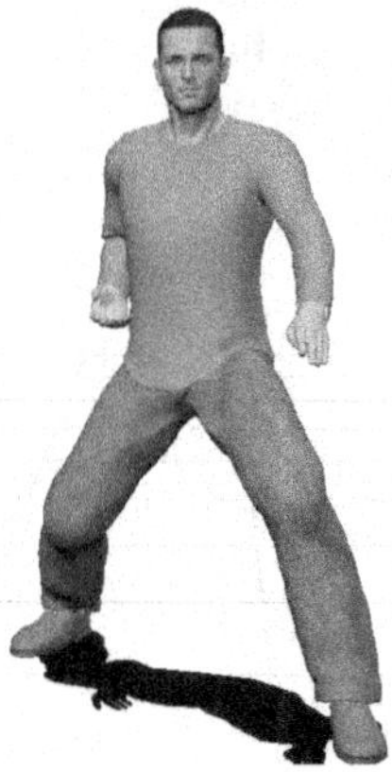

When moving into the high block on the next move bring the hand up the centerline of the body with the palm turned inwards.

This motion aligns with the flow of energy from the tan tien, and the positioning of the central meridian. It will make the movement powerful and hard to stop.

A NOTE:

Whenever possible the hands should be turned prior to the final position, then snapping into the position. This will help the student learn how to snap all muscles into the movement at the same time. This is called 'Focus.'

The real principle behind focus is the concept called 'Loose-Tight.'

The whole body should be loose, then the whole body should be tight at the focus of the movement, the the whole body should be loose again.

Beginning students are encouraged to tighten the whole body. Advanced students are encouraged to tighten only their fist, or the body part being used.

Retract the left foot slightly as you assume a back stance. Simultaneously bring the left hand up the centerline to execute a left high knife hand block.

Step forward with the right foot into a front stance as you bring the left hand up the centerline to execute a right high knife hand block.

No Switch Step because the back stance has already set up the footwork.

Bring the right foot back for the switch step as you lower the right palm to a guard the face.

Side view of the last move.

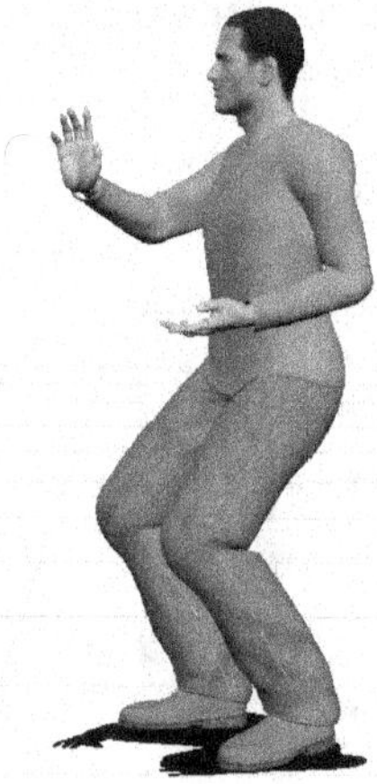

Step forward with the left foot with the left foot into a front stance as you bring the left hand up the centerline to execute a left high knife hand block.

Bring the left foot back for the switch step as you lower the left palm to guard the face.

Step forward with the right foot into a front stance as you bring the right hand up the centerline to execute a right high knife hand block.

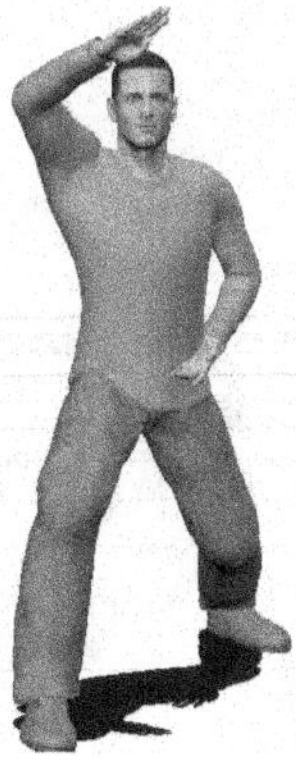

Execute a left reverse punch.
The punch should be done fast.
KIAI!

A NOTE:

The word 'Kiai' means 'spirit shout.'

It is not just a yell, it is a short, sharp bark that is filled with every ounce of intention.

A good Kiai can frighten an opponent.

A good Kiai increases the focus of a technique.

A good Kiai should erupt from the tan tien

If you are struck, a good Kiai makes you immune to pain and damage.

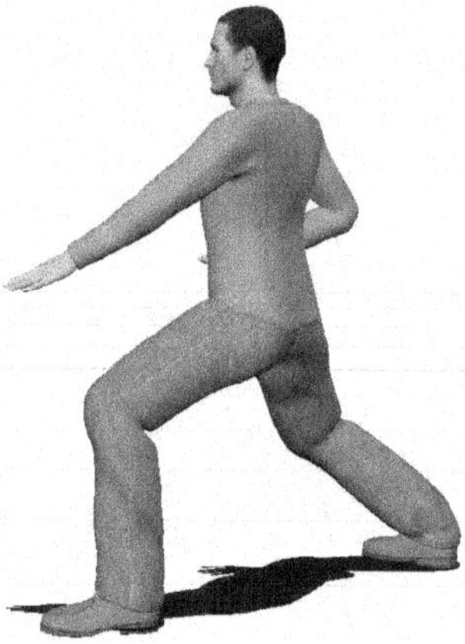

The next move is to execute a low block to the right in a front stance.

There are two ways to do this next move.

On the next page I will explain the original method, and describe the method I replaced it with.

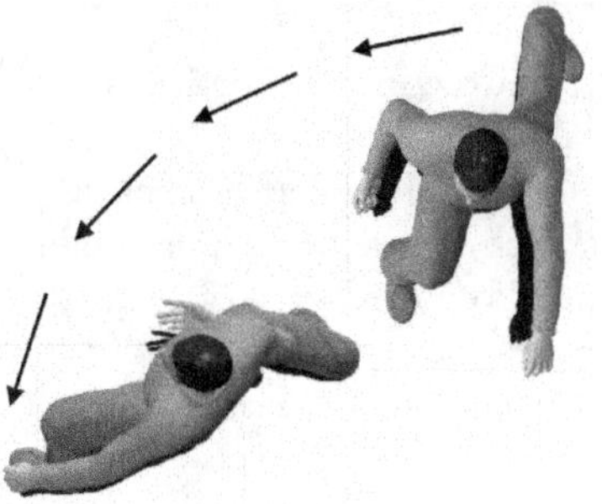

The original method was to launch yourself, spinning to the rear. The feet actually move 90 degrees, but the body turns 270 degrees.

In doing the original method you have to 'know' where you are going in order to 'peg' the stance and properly sink the weight and root the stance. There is a very 'zen' feeling to this move

However, while this is good for zen, it is not good for combat. The idea of stepping blindly to the rear in combat is abhorrent, in spite of the argument that the 'zen' intuition will protect you.

Thus, I prefer to step to the left with the right foot as in the images below. This moves you away from the attack, sets up the defense without danger of being blind while you turn your back on the opponent, and causes a shifting in the legs as you prepare to charge into the front stance that will develop into chi power.

This is actually a major change, and I like to tell people what the changes are and why I made them. I recommend that you do both changes and make up your mind as to which suits you. Or even better, do them both, alternating occasionally, so you get both the zen and the chi.

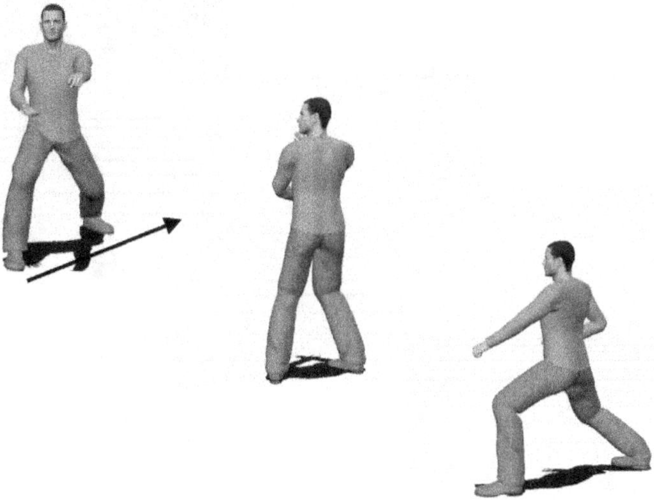

To continue the form…

Bring the left foot back in a switch step as you circle the left hand outward as if catching a punch.

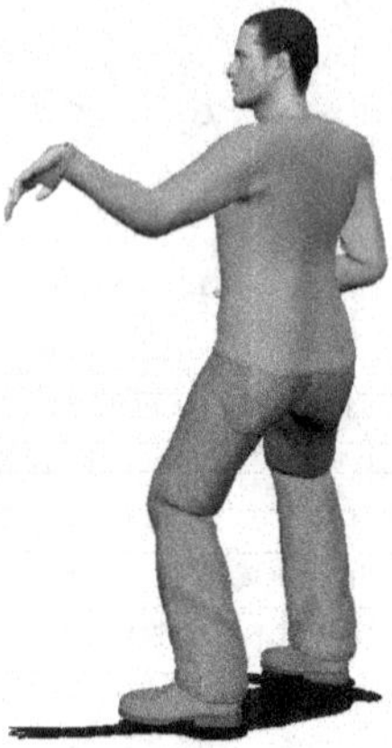

Step forward with the right foot into a Front Stance. The left arm should continue circling to the chamber position. The right hand should execute a lunging punch.

Bring the left foot up and begin a 180 degree turn to the right

Do a Switch Step on the turn (forward with the left, pivot, then forward with the right in the other direction) into a front stance as you execute a right low block.

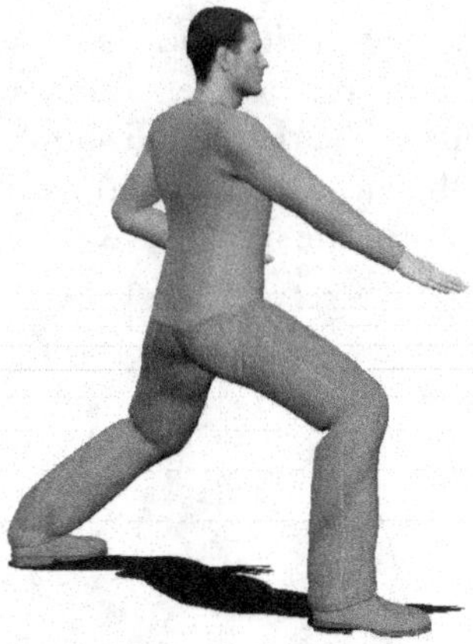

Bring the right foot back in a switch step as you circle the right hand outward as if catching a punch.

Step forward with the left foot into a front stance. The right should continue circling to the chamber position. The left hand should execute a lunging punch.

Retract the left foot as you pivot 90 degrees to the left into a cat stance. The right hand should guard the face while the left hand prepares for the next move.

Step forward with the left foot into a front stance as you execute a left low block.

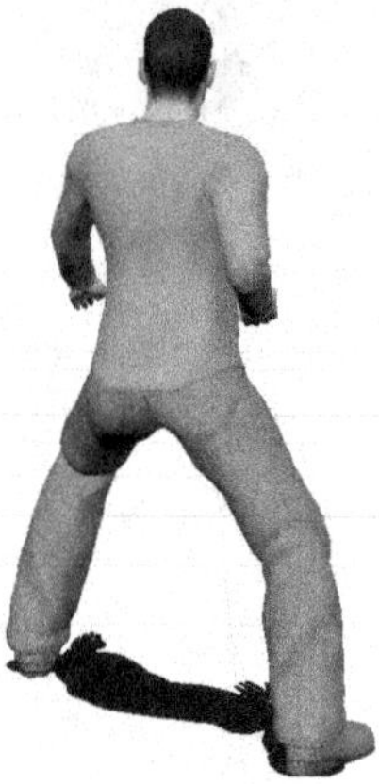

Bring the left foot back for the switch step as you circle the left hand outward as if guiding a punch.

Step forward with the right foot into a front stance. The left arm should continue circling to the chamber position. The right hand should execute a lunging punch.

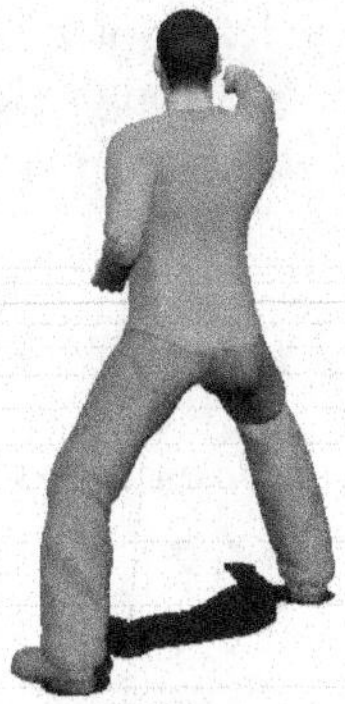

Bring the right foot back for the switch step. Circle the right hand outward

Step forward with the left foot into a front stance. The right arm should continue circling to the chamber position. The left arm should execute a lunging punch.

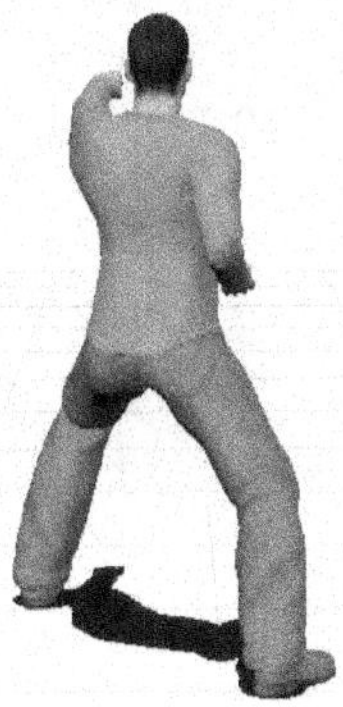

Bring the left foot back for the switch step as you circle the left hand outward as if catching a punch.

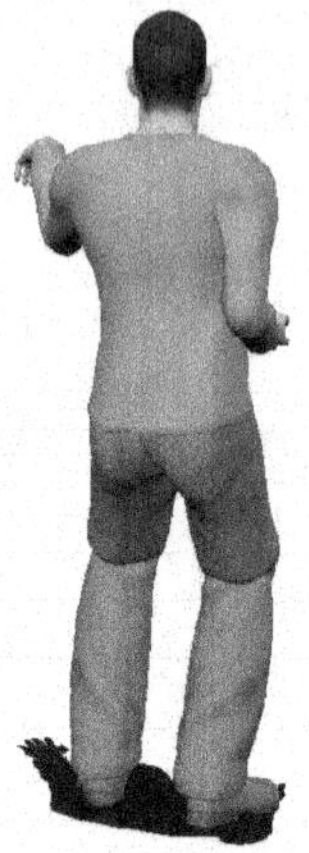

Step forward with the right foot into a front stance. The left arm should continue circling to the chamber position. The right arm should execute a lunging punch.

This move should be done fast.

KIAI!

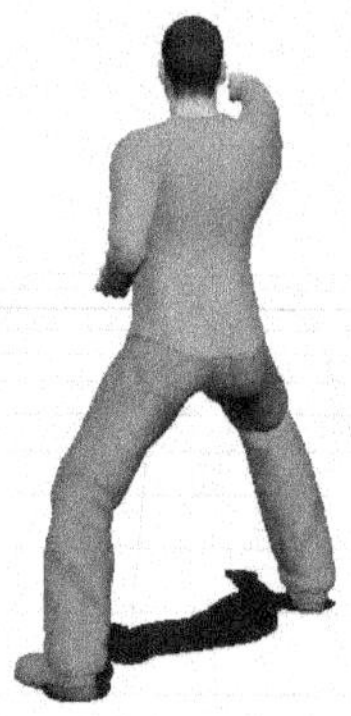

Pivot 180 degrees to the left along the line of the feet into a back stance. Simultaneously execute a left knife hand block.

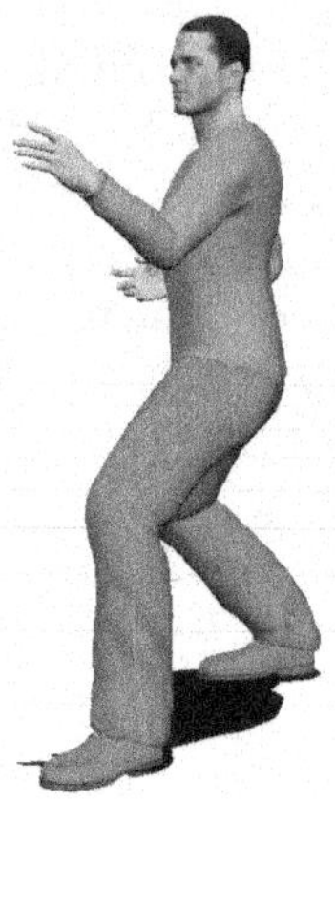

Pivot 180 degrees to the right into a back stance as you execute a right knife hand block.

Step 90 degrees to the left with the left foot into a back stance as you execute a left knife hand block.

Pivot 180 degrees to the right into a back stance as you execute a right knife hand block.

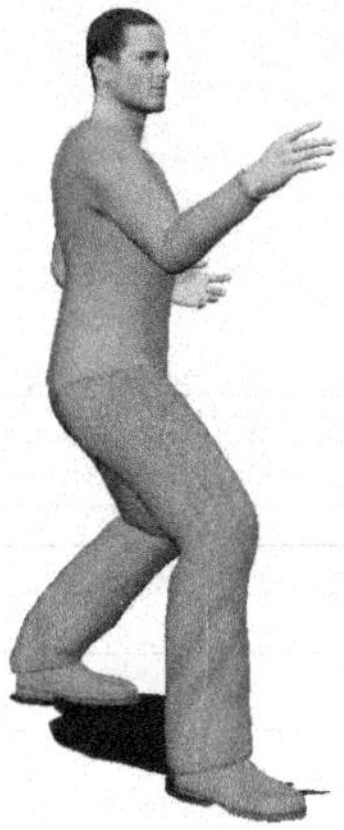

Return the left foot back to an hourglass stance, then assume a Natural stance in the same place you were when you began the form.

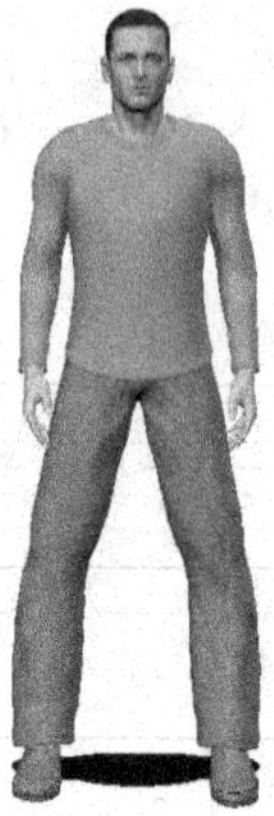

CHIANG NAN ONE

APPLICATION ONE

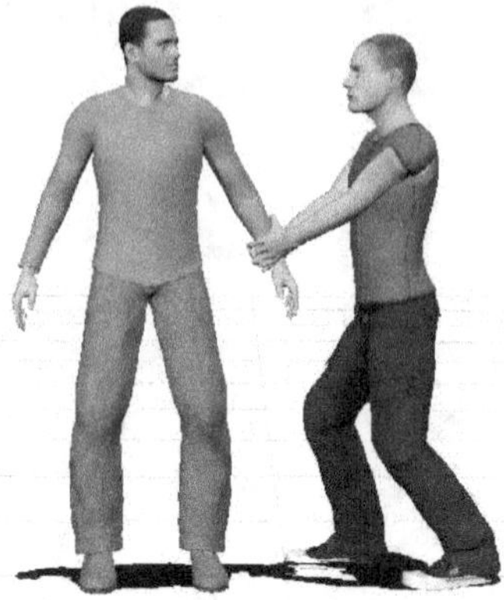

Let's look at the original concepts behind the Low Block.

I have never seen anybody do this one, though it is incredibly logical, and a direct application of the form that is good for combat.

Of course, it is also a technique that the old Okinawan Masters would take out of karate before ever teaching karate to children.

The Attacker grabs the wrist from the side with both hands.

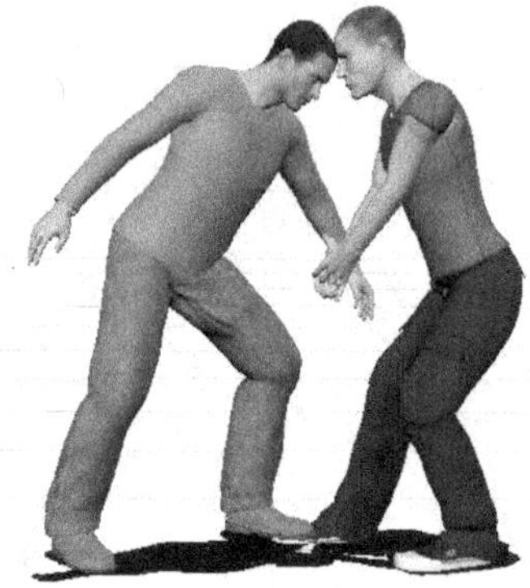

Actually, you can relax and do nothing at this point, for his hands are occupied and he is not in a position to attack.

But, let's say he has a friend coming, or there is some other reason for you to effect an escape.

Do the first move out of Chiang Nan One, step to the side with a low block, and lean into the technique to head butt the attacker.

He may let go at this point, but you never let up once you have decided to attack. Depending upon the distance, you may step forward with the left foot, or use a Switch Step to move the left foot forward, and push or punch the attacker backwards.

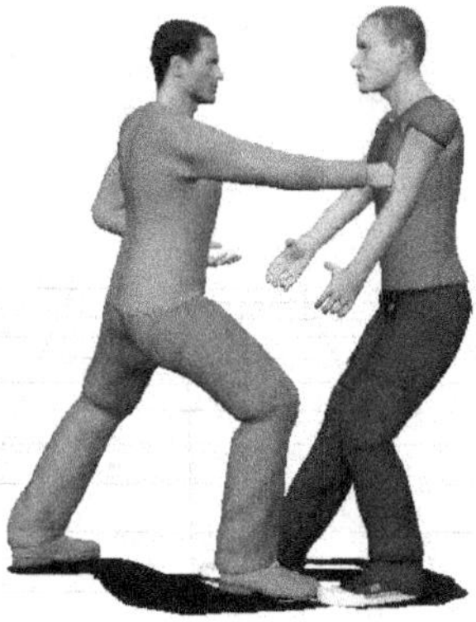

Done properly, he will go flying, or just lay down and cry.

WHAT'S WRONG WITH THE CLASSICAL LOW BLOCK!

On this page is an image of one person executing a low block on a kick. This is the classical technique, taught in almost every school. I want you to look at this picture. Take a few minutes. Think about it. Tell me what is wrong with it.

And, believe me, there is something wrong with it.

Make sure you have examined the image thoroughly…we will take it up on the next page.

You should not teach a beginner to block a kick with a forearm right away. The beginner has not toughened his arms, learned his timing, and the sad fact is that the thick bones and heavy mass of the leg can break the thinner bones and less mass of the arm.

Later on, when the student has made some progress, you can teach him this technique. The reason is simple: when a person gets near black belt he begins to realize that people have unique and separate notions of time. Thus, the expert will see the leg coming up, appreciate it as a unique motion, and utilize his own sense of time to break the leg as if it is a (relatively) unmoving, inanimate object.

To a black belt a body part is pretty much an inanimate object.

I know there will be people who object to what I say here, but this is only because Karate has degraded to the point where black belts no longer differentiate the separate universes (and time within those universes) and can no longer use their sense of time to impinge upon (over ride) another person's universe.

I know, what I said sounds like gobbledegook, but only if you haven't reached the state of mind of a true black belt.

The fact is that I have seen the low block, delivered with classic power, appropriate body alignment, correct CBM, break an attacker's leg in two places. That's right, one block…but two breaks. The block actually broke a chunk out of the bone, removed a section of bone.

On the next page we are going to go into the correct usage of the low block and how it was designed to be used. It is necessary to know this to get to the point where one can break a leg easily.

APPLICATION TWO

One problem with blocking a kick is that you are too far away to punch. After the block you have to step or shuffle forward. But stepping takes too long, and the back leg is extended, which means it isn't bent and ready to propel the body in a shuffle.

The proper use of a low block is for a punch to the mid section. Furthermore, you should block out of a back stance.

One can then utilize the bend (spring) of the back leg to move the whole body weight into the punch.

APPLICATION THREE

There is always a problem of executing a low block for a kick, but the kick is too low, which would necessitate the defender bending over and being out of position. If a person is trained how to block a leg too soon he may not be able to differentiate between a kick and a sweep or knee kick.

This is why we have the Switch Step.

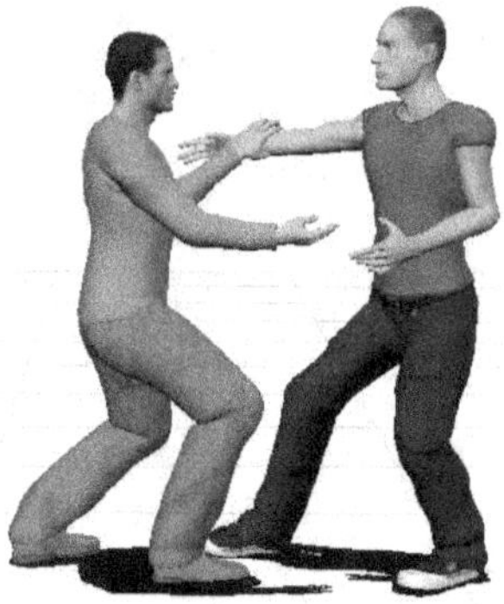

If an attacker kicks for the knee the defender moves the leg back and charges forward with the other leg.

If the attacker executes a punch mid technique (or even alone), this is why we have the outward circling hand motion in the punches.

The defender circles his arm and grabs the attacker's wrist on the way in. He pulls the wrist back (to his chamber position) pulling the attacker off balance, tying up his arms, and not letting him back away.

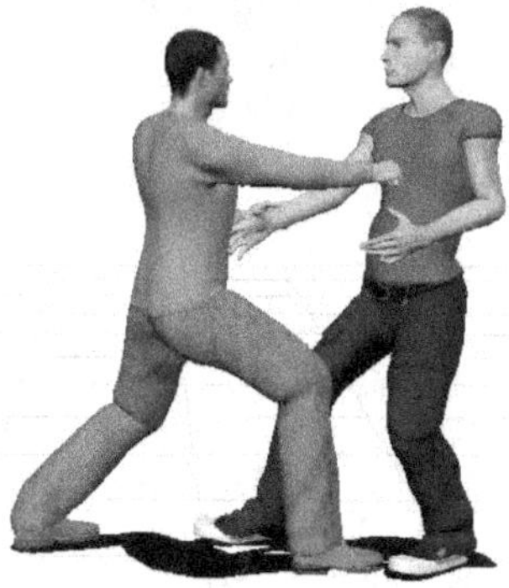

If somebody attacks you, you should NEVER let him get away. He will just try another attack.

The defender then pulls the attacker into his own punch, which increases the power.

APPLICATION FOUR

Another use of the switch step is for the kick attack.

As the attacker kicks (high or low), step half way back with the left foot as you block low, then step forward with the right foot as you execute a right punch.

Obviously, you will have to tailor this move to fit the circumstances, which brings us to an interesting point.

You should practice e the techniques as shown, try to make them work as shown.

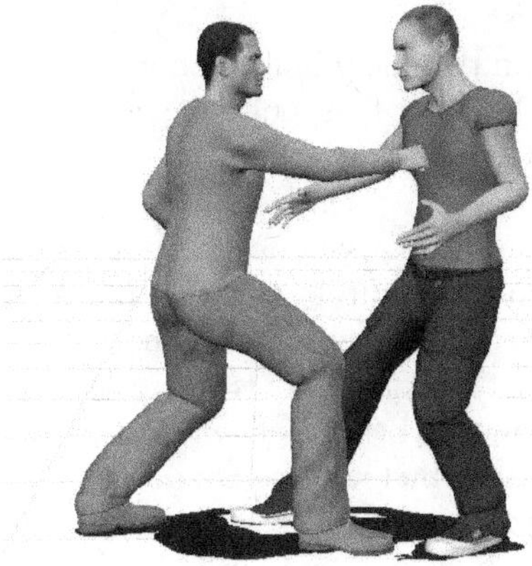

Then, having tried to apply the exact points of alignment, breathing, CBM, and so on, you can adapt.

There are three steps in the martial arts: the perfection of the form, the attempt to implement the pure concept of the form into the odd circumstance of reality. The final step would be to attempt to implement the pure concept into the chaos of combat.

And, a senior principle here: the more you work, the more reality will fit to your promise fight.

And I should define a Promise Fight here.

We called techniques taken from the forms 'Promise Fights.' They are the 'promise of a fight,' which is to say, they are an agreed upon concept, they are a postulate of motion about to be enacted.

Remember; nothing in the universe happens without a thought; there must be thought before action, and it is possible to 'see' these thoughts.

APPLICATION FIVE

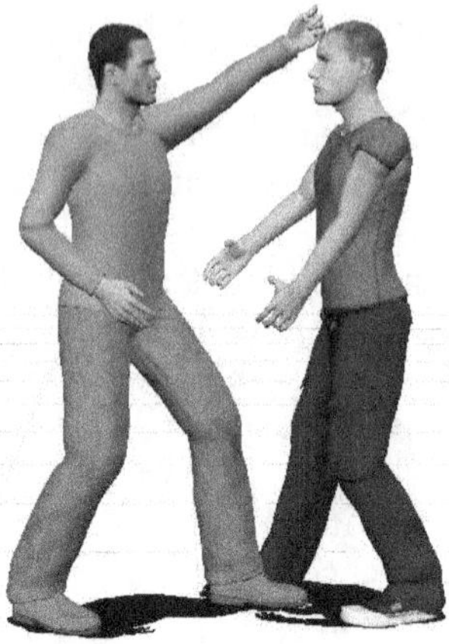

The third move of Chiang Nan One is a low block into a circling hammer fist to the head… or some other odd variation.

I shouldn't have to tell you how many things are wrong with this. To make a large arm circle before somebody gives a short punch is the least of the problems with this technique.

The real movement should be a quick and fast rolling of the fists at waist level.

In the Kang Duk Won we used hammer fists, but you should actually be rolling the fists.

We also defended against a kick and two low punches, striking the punches with the fists. Really sharpened our sense of timing.

At any rate, here is the real technique, which has been misplaced by the masters and undiscovered by the karate robots who follow masters blindly.

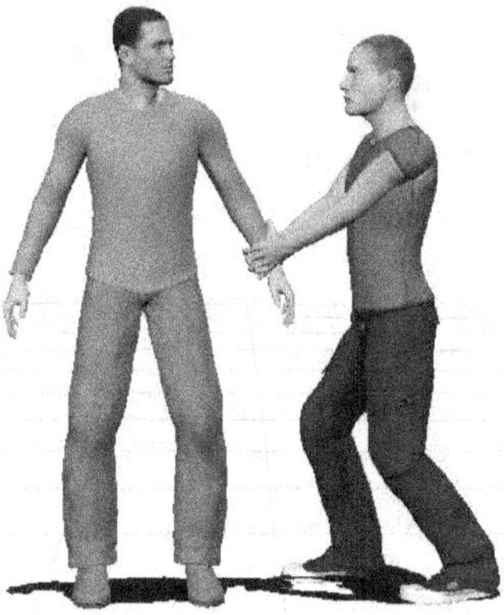

The attack is a simple two handed grab to the wrist from the side.

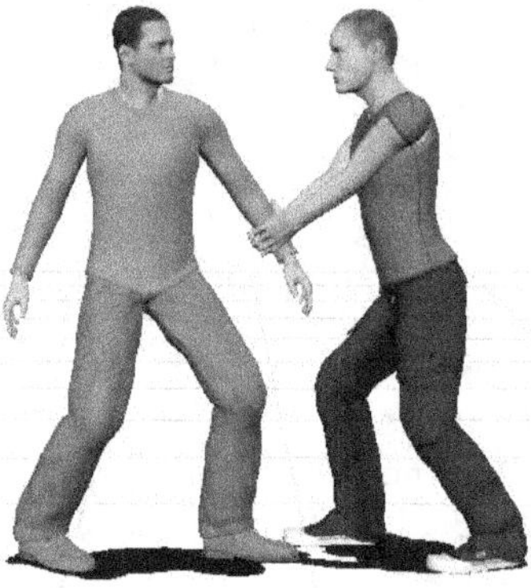

The defender steps slightly away, utilizing his whole body weight to pull the attacker off balance.

Turning and sinking into a backlist the defender strikes the attacker left hand with his right fist.

The attacker's right hand should be broken, seriously, and the defender rolls the left hand out of the attacker's right grab and punches the wrist.

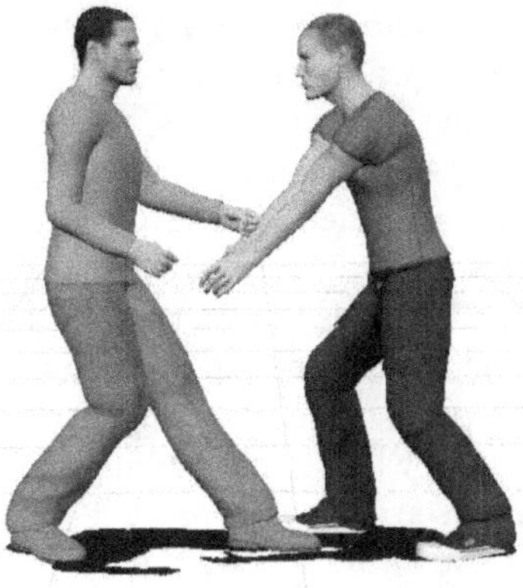

The defender then steps forward with the left foot into a front stance, putting his entire body weight into a punch to the attacker's chest.

The attacker should have a broken chest and be thrust firmly away.

I mention the broken chest, because though the old Master's may have been mistaken in passing down the art, they still had to train they could split the lacquered armor Japanese troops wore.

APPLICATION SIX

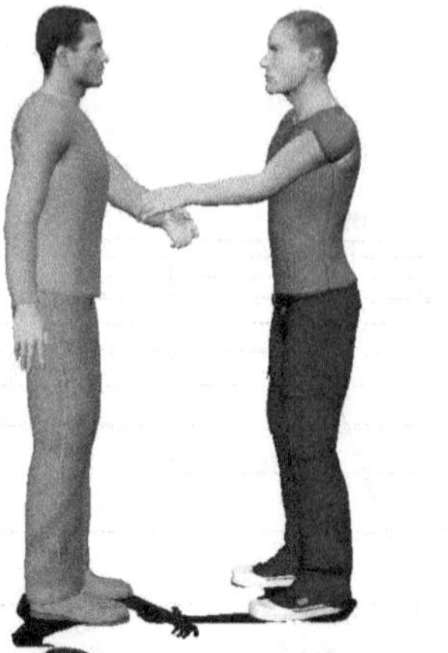

The attacker grabs the defenders left wrist with his left hand.

The attacker clamps the attacker's hand in place with his right hand and snakes his left hand under and then over the attacker's wrist.

There are many methods of doing this.

Move the snaking hand as if cutting down the attacker's centerline with a sword.

My favorite: point at the attacker's tan tien with your index finger.

And there are other methods.

The most important thing is to not press on the attacker's wrist, but to 'crawl' over it, cranking the attacker's arm.

You know you are doing it right when the attacker's knees buckle suddenly, or he stomp one foot (counting like a horse).

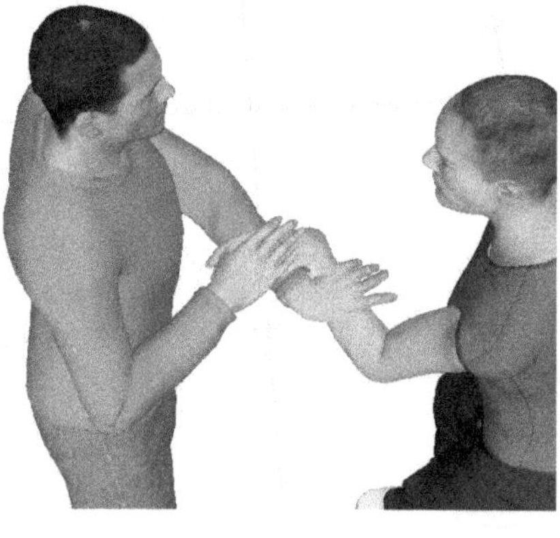

APPLICATION SEVEN

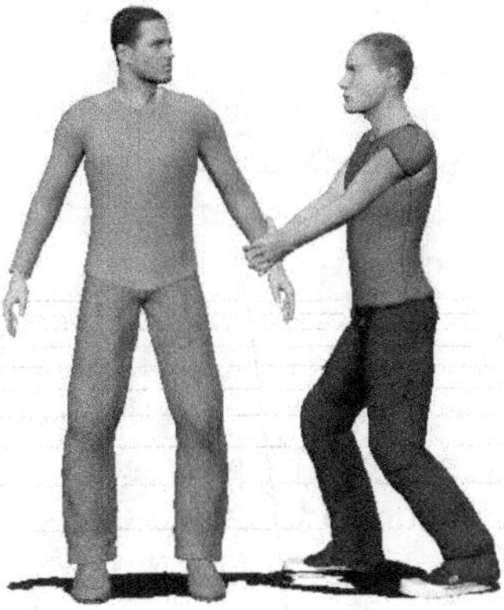

The attacker grabs the defenders left wrist with two hands from the side.

The defender pivots and sinks his weight as he drives the left hand down and scoops it to the right.

The attacker might be able to hold the wrist, but he can't hold the entire body weight, which is what he is holding when the hips are dropped, thus, the grab is broken.

The defender steps/shifts forward into a front stance as he executes a left high block.

The high block drives under the chin, snapping the head back and exposing the body for a right reverse punch.

Or, one could simple transform the high block into an elbow strike to the face.

Or, one could circle the left hand, grab the attacker's left wrist, and pull him into down as he executes a right punch.

Obviously, there are lots of options, and all options should be explored until the technique is understood no matter what might happen.

APPLICATION EIGHT

A simple, classical technique with some unstated concepts.

The Attacker steps forward and punches to the face with the right hand.

The defender steps back with the right foot into a back stance as he executes a left high block.

The defender steps/shifts into a front stance as he executes a punch.

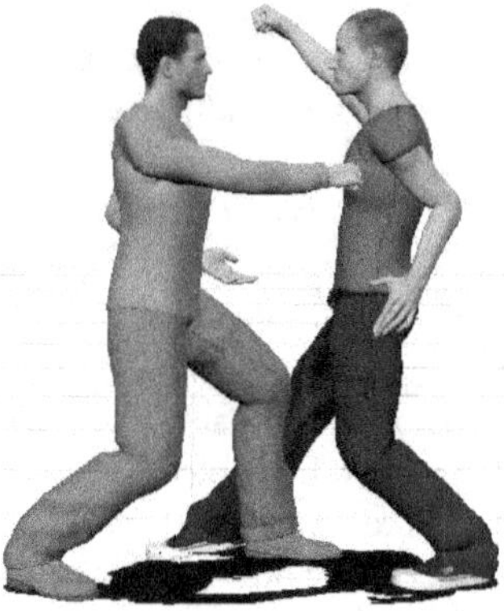

What instructors don't understand, or at least don't describe, are the three elements of power.

When you move forward into the punch you are THRUSTING the entire body body.

When you turn the hips you are ROTATING the body weight.

When you land on the front foot you are dropping your weight.

Thus, there are three elements of power.

Combine these elements of power so they are utilized to the correct degree in each technique, and back them up with correct breathing, relaxation, body alignment and CBM, and you will have internal power. It is that simple.

A good basic practiced endlessly is the secret of the martial arts.

And, there are no advanced techniques without polished basics.

APPLICATION NINE

Attacker kicks with the right foot.

Defender shoots his right leg back and drops his weight down into a front stance, and a left low block onto the Attacker's ankle.

A broken leg should result.

If the leg isn't broken, and the attacker puts his right foot down and punches to the face with his right hand, the defender shifts back into a back stance and executes a left high block.

The Defender grips the attacker's right wrist and pulls it to his side, tilting and off balancing the defender, as he shifts forward and strikes the attacker.

One thing you should consider is to explore techniques from all angles.

If the attack is a grab from the front, try a grab from the side, or the rear, or the other side.

Find out what you have to do, no matter the circumstance, to make the technique work in all possible scenarios.

And, a note: a grab attack is good training, but you should eventually be performing your defense before the grab reaches you; a grab that hasn't reached you is just like a punch.

APPLICATION TEN

An interesting promise fight is to simple charge forward and beat the attacker to the punch, and simply 'override' any attack he is offering.

It's a good idea to bump his knee with your knee and knock him off balance in any technique.

APPLICATION ELEVEN

Another interesting Promise Fight is to hook the attacking hand and guide it to the side as you change the high block into a 'hook punch.'

This might entail a Switch Step, it might not.

APPLICATION TWELVE

Then there is the simultaneous block and counter.

Techniques should progress:
block and counter
same hand block and counter
simultaneous B & C.

The instructor should be careful to lead the student through these progressions in a gradient manner as the abilities accumulate.

APPLICATION THIRTEEN

The attacker steps forward with the right foot and punches to the face with the left hand.

The defender steps back with the right foot into a back stance as he executes a right cross palm block.

The attacker punches to the face with the right hand.

The defender pivots the hips slightly to the right as he executes a left high block.

The defender steps/shifts forward into a front stance as he pulls the attacker's right hand with his left hand and a right punch to the face.

The good instructor should take the student through the following progression:

one attack ~ one B & C
two attacks ~ two Bs & C
three attacks ~ three Bs& C

I used to apply this progression through the stages of belts.

White belt ~ one attack
Green belt ~ two attacks
Brown belt ~ three attacks

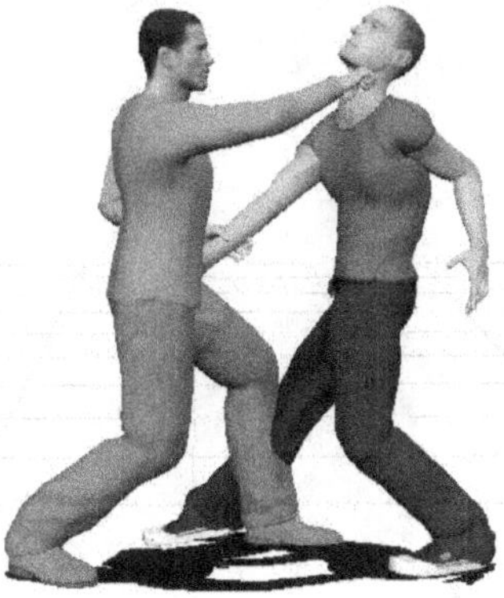

And, of course, the grab arts at the end of the technique should grow progressively more vicious.

APPLICATION FOURTEEN

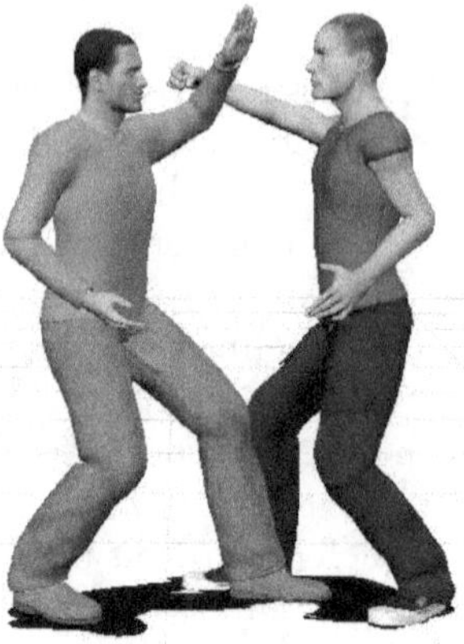

Here's a very clever promised fight that nobody knows.

The attackers steps forward with the right foot and punches to the face with the right hand.

The defender steps back with the right foot into a back stance as he executes a right high block.

The defender then punches down with the left hand, the same hand he used to block, into the joint between the thigh and the waist.

The attacker will crumple.

Be careful of head butting. Or not.

I tend to simply use a spear hand, using the tips of my fingers to press downward.

APPLICATION FIFTEEN

After executing the knife hand block the defender can turn the knife hand into a grab and pull the attacker's arm while he strikes him in the face with the left hand.

Many people sneer at the tendency of karate students to retract one hand to the chamber position when punching with the other hand.

Actually, there are several good reasons for this 'chambering' or 'cocking' of the hand.

The body is balanced; one hand goes out and the other comes in.

The hands are being utilized with the lines of energy emanating from the tan tien in mind.

You can argue about these sorts of reasons, or not, as you wish.

The real reason, as depicted in the image above, is that you are not merely withdrawing your hand, you are grabbing and pulling the attacker's wrist so that he is pulled off balance, can't get away, and drawn into an outgoing force that will become, for his forward momentum, that much more powerful.

APPLICATION SIXTEEN

After executing the knife hand block the defender can turn the knife hand into a grab and pull the attacker's arm while he executes a left front snap kick to the groin with the left foot.

APPLICATION SEVENTEEN

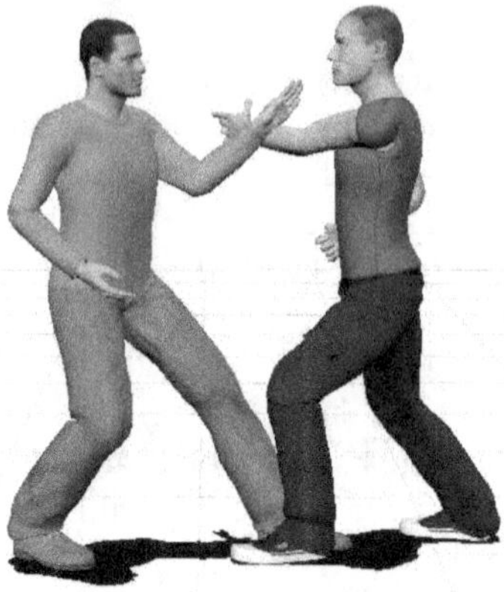

The attacker steps forward with the left foot and punches to the face with the left hand.

The defender steps back with the right foot into a back stance as he executes a knife block.

The defender stabs to the eyes with the left hand, the same hand he blocked with.

Whether it is a single knife hand block or double knife hand block depends on what technique is being executed, but can be based just on preference.

Follow up strikes are dictated by which way the attacker's body moves.

It is said that no technique ends in a block.

Thus, as you can see in the preceding techniques, the knife hand is not just a block.

And, I will say that there there can be, occasionally, exceptions to the rule. Enjoy the next technique, which ends with a block.

APPLICATION EIGHTEEN

The attacker steps forward with the right foot and punches to the face with the right hand.

Defender steps slightly forward and slightly to the left with the left foot as he executes a left cross palm block.

The defender pushes the attacker's arm across his body, trapping it, as he steps behind the attacker's right foot with his left foot and executes a left low block.

The attacker is swept back over the defender's foot to a fall.

This technique should not be taught until the attacker knows how to do a break fall from a waist high position. He can't simply squat down and roll backwards, he is going to go down from two or three feet flat on his back.

This is a 'splitting' technique, the top of the body goes one way, the bottom of the body goes the other way.

Technically, it is a Monkey Boxing technique, but one thing I've learned is that if you do the art long enough, if you search deep enough, every technique can be found in every art.

CONCLUSION TO THE PROMISE FIGHTS OF CHIANG NAN ONE

When you do thee preceding techniques do them on each side.

Always start slow, and pick up speed only when the technique is familiar. Remember the Injury Formula.

Speed + Ignorance = Injury

Play with whether a technique can be made to work on the opposite side for which it is designed.

Play with which foot is forward, which hand is forward.
There are four potentials here.

right foot forward with the right hand forward
right foot forward with the left hand forward
left foot forward with the left hand forward
left foot forward with the right hand forward

Keep track of which techniques work in which situations, and always remember the most important truth:

You always learn more from mistakes,
but only if you're intelligent enough to see them.

Chapter Four
Chiang Nan Two

Below are the videos for form Two.

channan 2 ~https://youtu.be/C-NUneyZ1l8	1:54
channan 2 side ~ https://youtu.be/gk_Cah9NNM0	1:37
channan 2 explained ~ https://youtu.be/ETaUmsmBUCc	10:18
channan 2 app 8 ~ https://youtu.be/-uS48cBR1w8	7:17
channan 2 app 9 ~ https://youtu.be/qVisVSrHfDs	5:52
channan 2 app 10 ~ https://youtu.be/7o5k3XdrwNQ	6:12
channan 2 app 11 ~ https://youtu.be/80JZA6MgnNs	5:06
channan 2 app 12 ~ https://youtu.be/QkFaFl3UGFA	4:39
channan 2 app 13 ~ https://youtu.be/bUNmfJeqMcI	5:45
channan 2 app 14 ~ https://youtu.be/Vf-0pqhOK2o	4:22
channan 2 app 15 ~ https://youtu.be/xMCzn6uCASo	6:36
	43:44

Chiang Nan Two

All too often we hear that this art is sacred, that art must never be changed, anything that was passed down to us is inviolate.

Rubbish.

"Even in the forty years that I have been practicing Karate, the changes have been many. It would be interesting to be able to go back in time, to the point when the kata were created, and study them." ~ Shigeru Egami (founder of Shotokai Karate)

And it was Gichin Funakoshi who said, 'To search for the old is to understand the new.'

So, with the knowledge that everything has changed, let's look back to the roots, let's see if we can understand it all anew.

Okinawa is been the gateway to the orient. For its entire history countries have established embassies there. Cultures have come and gone, and Okinawa has been the better for it.

In particular, Okinawa has long been a hotbed of martial arts. Cultures coming and doing, the unrest of an always boring culture, the constant threat of invasion by the two countries who claimed they 'owned' Okinawa (Japan and China), the study of the martial arts was constant and intense.

One master of Karate was Anko Itosu (1831-1916). Itosu studied Te (literally 'hand,' the name for karate in those early days) with many of the masters of the day.

There are many versions concerning the birth of Karate, but the most common, and probably the most trustworthy, is that a Chinese sailor was shipwrecked on the coast of Okinawa. He sought shelter in a cave outside a cemetery located near Tomari.

Itosu is said to have met (befriended?) the sailor, and the fellow shared his martial arts with Itosu.

The name of the form the sailor taught Itosu was Chiang Nan (also called Channan).

This may have been the name of the sailor, or perhaps the district the sailor was from (Jiangnan).

Itosu took the one long form of Chiang Nan and translated it into five shorter forms: the Pinans.

Chiang Nan, or Channan, was translated into Pinan, both words supposedly meaning 'Peaceful Mind,' in some sense.

Later, Gichin Funakoshi would rename the Pinan forms as 'Heian.'

The Pinan forms became the curriculum for Karate on Okinawa. Many systems used them for training, and, as time went on, many versions of these forms evolved.

The forms were used extensively by the bodyguards for the emperor of Okinawa, and the art reached a high level with the bodyguards.

Eventually, Japan decided to put an end to the clash with China over the ownership of Okinawa. To do so they ordered (kidnapped?) the emperor to live in Japan.

The bodyguards were left with no body to guard, and with no livelihood.

Some of them became merchants, some of them became teachers, and so on.

In 1908 the Pinans were utilized in the Okinawan educational system, and in this utilization was perhaps the greatest change to the art.

Nobody would want to have their children learn how to head butt and eye gouge, nobody wanted murder and mayhem committed over lunch money, so the Pinans were watered down, made into a less vicious form of physical exercise.

In the early 1920s some of the Okinawan martial artists went to Japan. They gave demonstrations, and some of them, most notably Gichin Funakoshi, opened schools and taught the Japanese.

But would the Okinawans, even if they knew the true techniques of Karate, teach the people who had stolen their emperor?

The answer is no. In 'Hidden Karate' by Higaki (pen name), on page 65, it is revealed that the Okinawan Karate masters made a secret pact not to teach the real Karate.

They would teach the forms, the forms that had already been watered down for school children, but they wouldn't teach the real forms, and certainly not the fighting techniques of those 'Chiang Nan' forms.

Thus, to this day we have one new version of karate after another, even versions with no forms, and this is nothing but the attempt of the students, now masters in America, to discover the truth of Karate, of what had been hidden from them.

To be honest, while I have done much research, and am confident that I have uncovered much of what was hidden in that long ago pact, I don't pretend to teach the original Chiang Nan kata.

And actually, I don't think I would want to.

After all, even if I could hop into a time machine, go back in time and recover the original form of that lost kata, who is to say that that that kata is nothing more than the victim of another secret pact. Perhaps the Chinese made a secret pact that they would not teach the real kata to the Okinawans.

I say that with a smile, and a rude appreciation for history, and for the short-sightedness of people who make secrets.

I use matrixing to research the movements of the body in self defense, in the discipline of the martial arts, and in that science I do find my answers.

That said, in this book I will delve into the precise nature of what I have come to believe are the original movements of the martial arts, and how they came to be.

I will go into the matrixing principles I used to explore the Pinans, and how I reverse engineered my way back to Chiang Nan.

If not before Chiang Nan.

That said, let's look at the second Pinan form. Let's see what I have done to that, and then you can have opinion as to whether I am a genius, or just another fool on an errand down a dark alley on a moonless night.

CHIANG NAN TWO

Stand in the natural stance, able to move in any direction without 'pre-leaning.'

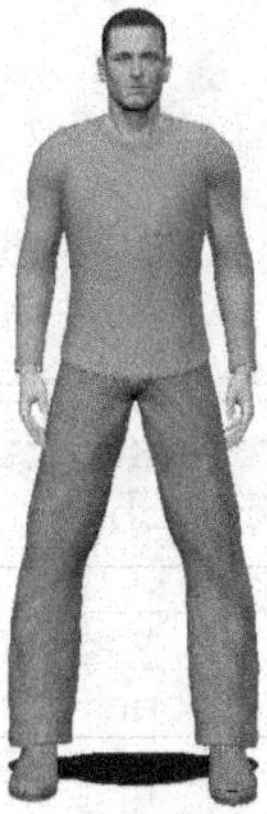

Step forward with the right foot and begin turning 90 degrees to the left. the hands should cross, then open.

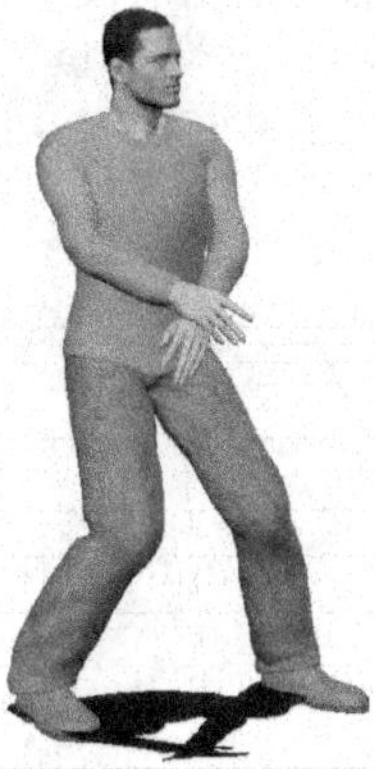

Sink into a back stance.
The left arm is at mid level, the right arm is at high level.

NOTE

There is much confusion concerning this 'mid/high' posture.

People just raise the arms, instead of bringing them close to the centerline and popping them.

People insist the top arm must be parallel to the ground.

And the confusions increase as the applications are considered.

If you are locked into the 'closed fist for every nearly application' mind set this contributes to the problem. It locks people into a certain mode.

For instance: you can only punch; you can only use explosive power.

I prefer the open hands, and for a reason.

The first two moves of the martial arts are slap, then grab, then block.

Blocking is the third in this sequence of motion.

Thus, most forms of karate are two steps behind because of the insistence upon closing the fist.

Closing the fist trains one to snap the fist, helps focus, but it is still a training device for the young.

I can easily see the old Okinawan masters changing the Pinans to closed fist forms so they don't have to get into explanations. They were taking the easy way out.

Unfortunately, most instructors take the easy way out, and this for a reason.

They don't understand the slap/grab potential.

Or, they have come up with bushwah reasons for what they are doing.

For instance, in the splayed feet stance of Goju: 'Pointing the feet outward this will 'soften' the back.'

But why would somebody soften the back? What is the purpose? The spine should actually be straightened, with the hips tucked for alignment.

The sad fact is that if somebody doesn't understand something they will say something this, or, my favorite: 'It builds chi,' ignoring totally body alignment and the scientific reasons behind correct alignment.

Roll the left arm inward and bring the right arm down in a parry. Make sure you square the hips as you do this.

One of the arms should change direction, but there is an overall fluidity and flow to this.

Continue the parry, retracting it towards the body. The left hand goes forward with a palm up spear. This is called 'White Snake (Spits Out Tongue) ' in Tai Chi Chuan.

Make sure you turn the hips to the right to align the body with the strike.

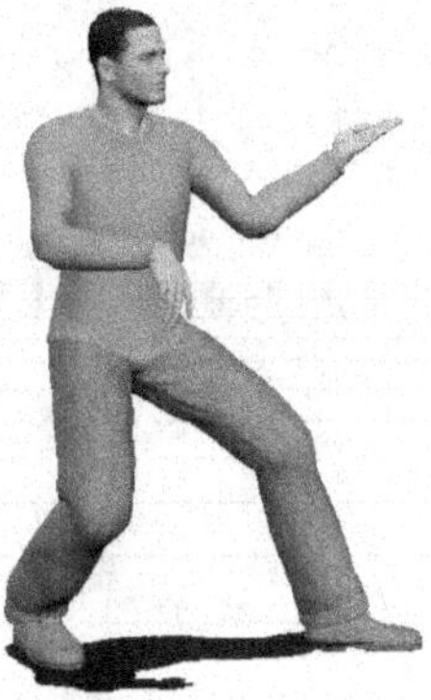

Snap the fist (spear hand).

Make sure the hips turn a last little bit to support the strike.

Punching off the back leg is called 'Pole Punching.'

The back leg is the dominate pole in the motor of the body.

Pivot to the right 180 degrees.

Bring the hands together, then open them.

Sink into a back stance as you execute a mid/high blocking position.

I say block, but having open hands gives more potentials.

Fold the right hand inward and down.

Bring the left hand down in parry.

Align the hips.

Extend the left hand in a palm up spear.

Retract the parry.

Align the hips.

Snap the fist (spear hand).

Beginners are taught to snap the whole body.

But whole body tension slows motion.

Thus, as soon as possible, the student should be taught to snap just the body part doing the work, and rely on correct body alignment and CBM
(Coordinated Body Motion) for power.

Doing CBM this way doesn't require you to develop 'chi power,' you instantly have it.

Bring the left foot forward.

Bring the right hand across the body.

The knees should remain bent.

Straighten up as you look to the right.

Move the left foot slightly to the side and turn it to the right as you begin circling the hands clockwise

Side view of last image.

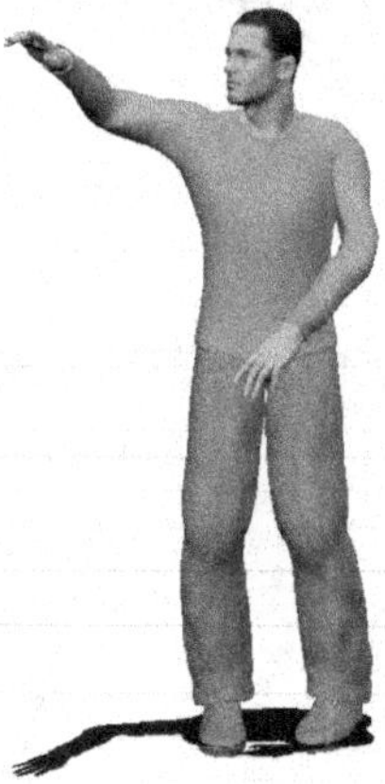

Pivot 90 degrees to the right as you continue to circle the hands.
The left hand should guard the face with a cross palm block, the right hand should guard the groin with a lower palm.

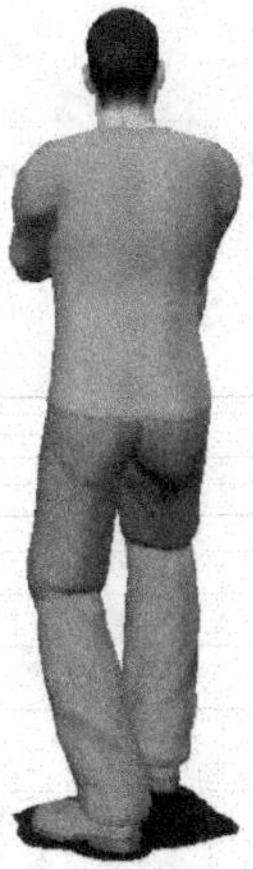

Side view of last image.

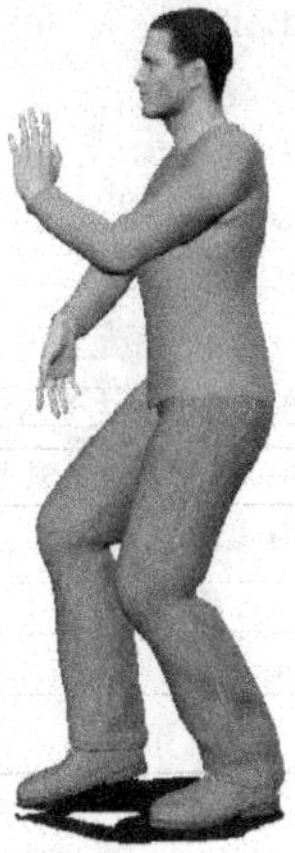

Execute a left mid level block and a right front snap kick.
The block should lock momentarily, the kick should snap. This is because of the motion involved in the next movement.
Palm up is a block; palm down is a grab. I do it both ways depending on what kind of energy I am putting into the form (karate or Tai Chi) or what application I am doing (blocking or grabbing).

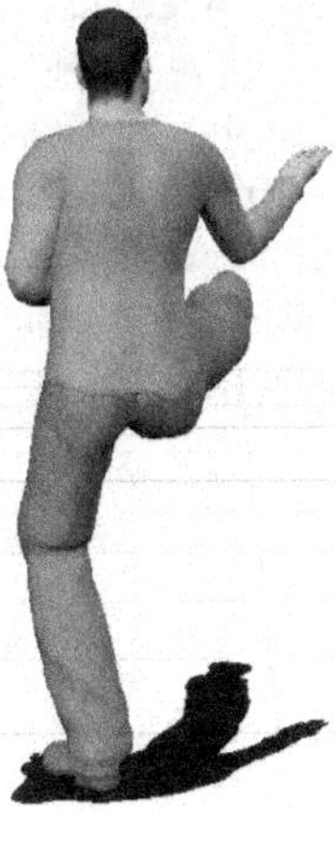

Side view of last image.

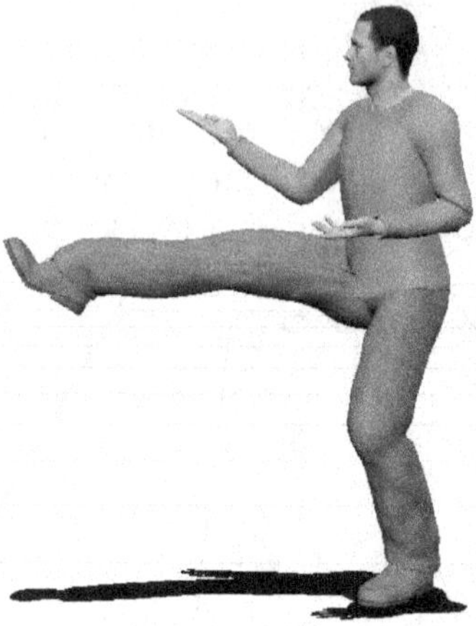

Turn 180 degrees and stomp the right foot as you shoot the left foot forward and assume a back stance.

At the same time execute an outward grabbing block (or double knife hand block).

This is a 'replacement movement. The right foot, when it stomps, lands in the exact spot the left foot was occupying.

NOTE ON SUPERCHARGING

Weight = work = energy.

To increase energy (chi power) utilize a lower stance, support more weight and the body has to work harder.

Stomping the foot as done in this last move causes a sudden increase of weight, which causes the tan tien to explode with more energy.

This is called 'supercharging.'

Do not stomp hard, just quick and fast. You do not want to overdo it and damage the foot.

Side view of last image.

Bring the left foot back and to the side (triangle step) and execute a Buddha Palm block with the left hand.

The Buddha palm is the slap in the 'slap grab' sequence we are executing.

Move the right foot forward and assume a back stance as you retract the left hand and execute a right outward grabbing block (or single knife hand block).

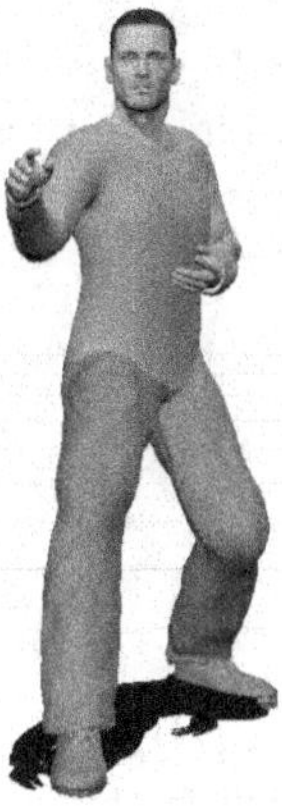

Bring the right foot back and to the side (triangle step) as you execute a buddha palm block with the right hand.

Move the left foot forward and assume a back stance as you retract the right hand and execute a left outward grabbing block (or single knife hand block).

Bring the left foot back and to the side (triangle step) as you execute a buddha palm block and with the left hand.

Move the right foot forward and assume a back stance as you retract the left hand and execute a right outward grabbing block (or single knife hand block).

Step/shift forward into a front stance as you execute a right palm (down) block and a left horizontal spear hand.

Traditionally, the spear hand is vertical. I don't strike people with the spear hand, I 'insert' the hand and press. Here I turn the hand for an actual strike to the throat.

Side view of last image.

Step forward and 45 degrees to the right with the left foot into a back stance as you execute a left outward grabbing block (or double knife hand block).

Pivot 180 degrees into a back stance as you execute a right knife hand block.

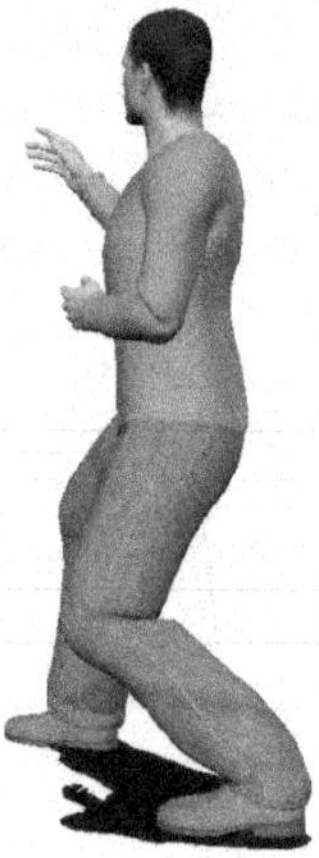

Step forward and 45 degrees to the left with the left foot into a back stance as you execute a left outward grabbing block (or double knife hand block).

Step back with the left foot and pivot 180 degrees to the left into a back stance as you execute a left outward grabbing block (or double knife hand block).

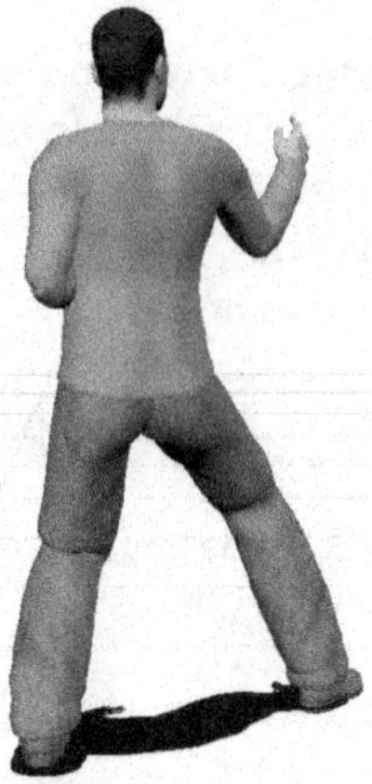

Retract the left foot as you lower the left hand.

Move the left foot 90 degrees to the left. The left hand circles clockwise to execute a palm block.

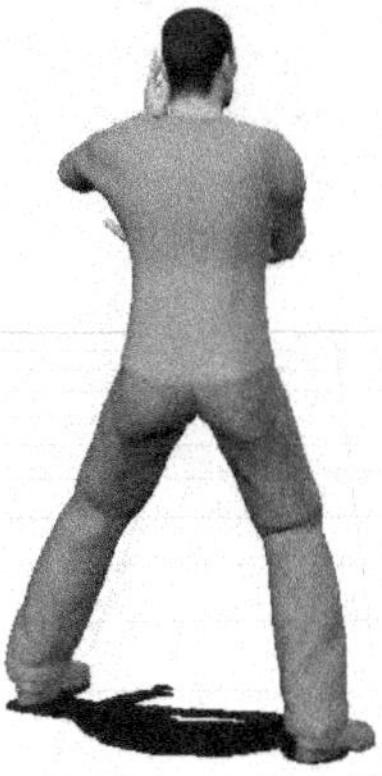

Keeping the feet in place, pivot the body to the left as you execute a right mid level outward grabbing block.

The hips should be twisted so as to give support to the right arm. The right foot should be pointing at the left foot.

It is okay to drag the right foot slightly forward.

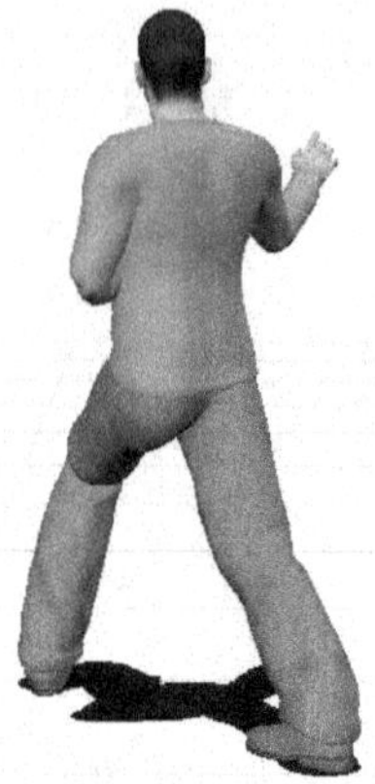

Execute a right front snap kick.

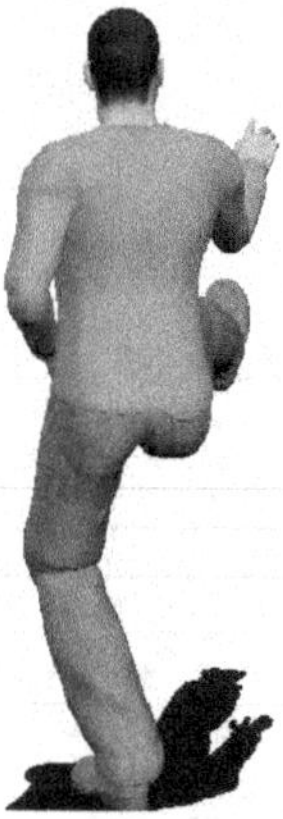

Set the right foot down in a front stance as you execute a left spear hand (sudden snap of the hand at last moment).

Keeping the feet in place, begin twisting the body to the right.

Circle the hands through a left upper cross palm block and a left cross palm block.

Side view of last image.

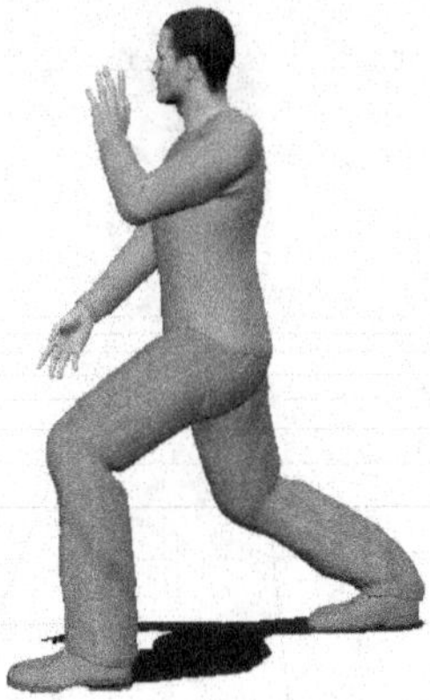

Twist the body to the right as you circle the hands to execute a left outward mid level grabbing block.

It is okay to drag the right foot slightly forward.

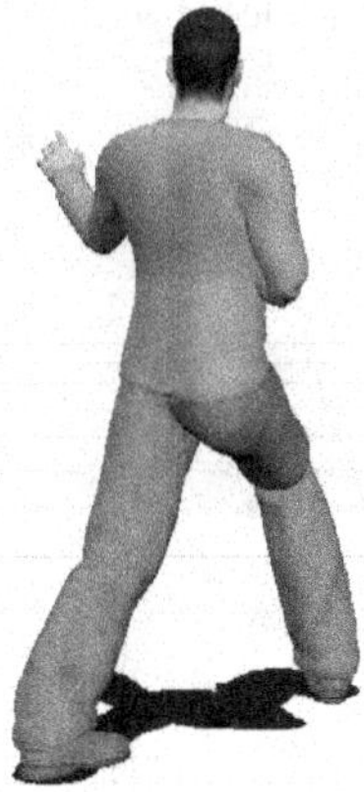

Execute a left front snap kick.

Set the left foot down in a front stance as you execute a right spear hand (sudden snap of the hand at the last moment).

Bring the left foot back (switch step) as you circle the hands clockwise. The right hand should guard the face, the left hand should guard the groin.

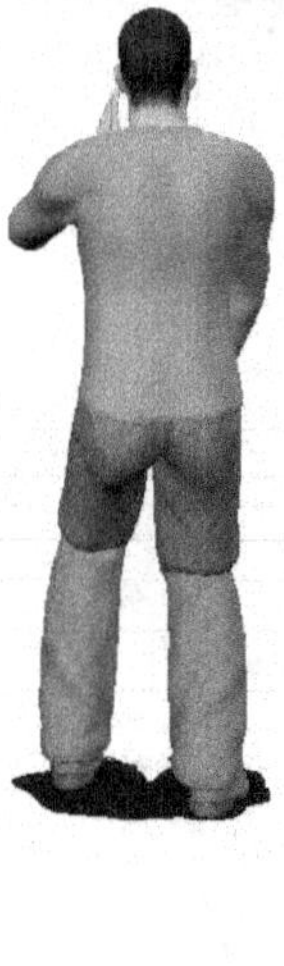

Step forward with the right foot into a front stance as you execute a right outward middle level grabbing block.

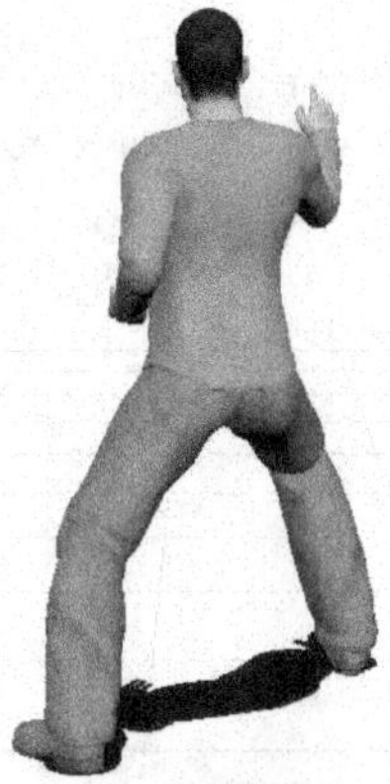

Bring the left foot forward into a cat stance as you pivot 45 degrees to the left. simultaneously execute a right Buddha Palm block.

Step forward with the left foot into a front stance as you execute a left low block.

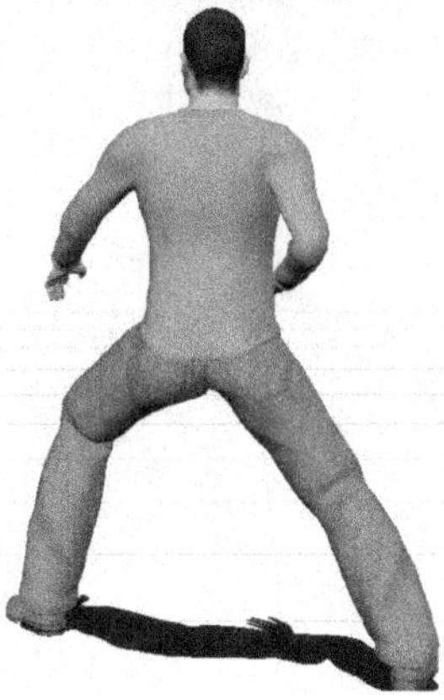

Bring the right foot up to the left (thru a cat stance) and turn 45 degrees to the right.

The left hand should guard the face.

Step forward with the right foot into a front stance as you execute a right high knife hand block.

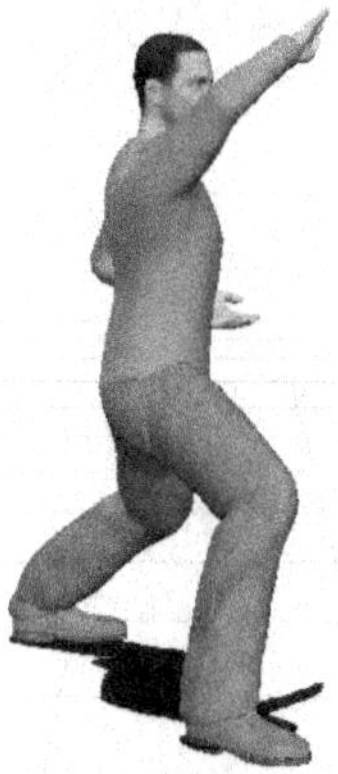

Bring the left foot up and pivot 90 degrees to the left into a cat stance as you execute a right Buddha Palm block

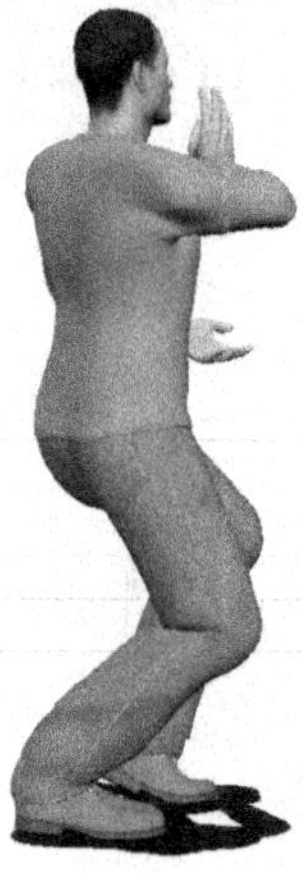

Step forward with the left foot into a front stance as you execute a left low block.

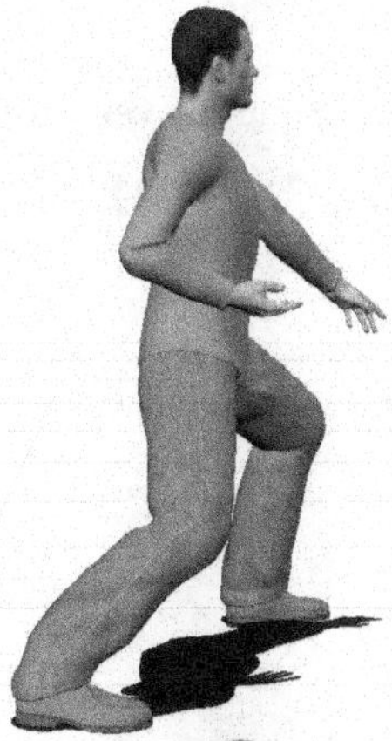

Pivot 180 degrees to the right into a cat stance as you execute left Buddha Palm block.

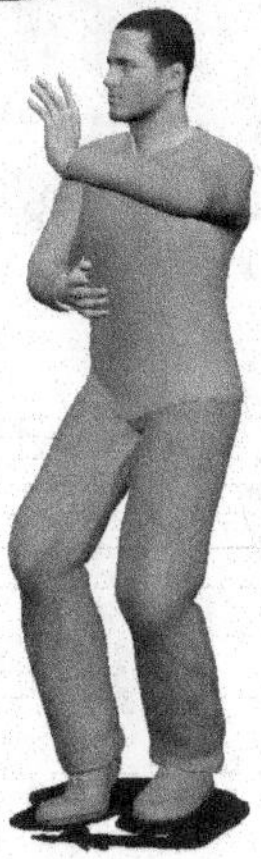

Step forward with the right foot into a front stance as you execute a right high block.

Execute a left reverse spear hand.

KIAI!

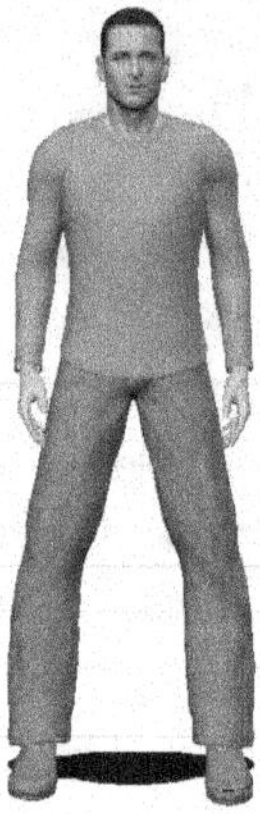

Return to the original position from which you began the form.

CHIANG NAN TWO

APPLICATION NINETEEN

Attacker steps forward with the right foot and punches with the right hand.

Defender steps back with the right foot into a back stance as he executes a mid/high block.

Attacker punches with the left hand.

Defender executes an inward middle level block.

Defender shuffles forward as he punches to the body with the right hand.

This is a 'hidden fist' technique, as the defender punches under the arms and is difficult for the attacker to see.

Pivot hips for each motion.

On the first move the power is down the back leg and the hips open to align the body.

On the second move the power is down the back leg and the hips rotate into the counter.

On the third move the power is down the back leg, with rotation of the hips and shuffling (thrusting) forward.

You should analyze EVERY move in this manner to make sure sinking the weight and body alignment are correct.

APPLICATION TWENTY

Attacker steps forward with the right foot and punches with the right hand.

The attacker punches to the face with the left hand.

The defender pivots to the right and executes a right high block.

The Attacker continues the high block, circling back and up (bolo punch) to strike under the attacker's floating rib.

The floating rib is not connected in the front, and easier to break, especially if you can angle your punch slightly upwards.

The attacker pivots into a horse stance and executes a hammer strike to the ribs.

NOTES

The bolo punch seems to be a far way to go, but practice and it will become very fast, and the power will be undeniable.

Striking off the back leg is sometimes held in disrepute by classical systems, but when you master 'pole punching' (rotating weight on the back leg), and feel the fragility of the attacker's body under your fists, you will understand that a back leg punch is not weak, only misunderstood.

There are three types of power: thrusting the whole body weight, rotating the hips (and therefore the body weight), and gravity (sinking the weight.

If you practice a system that only believes in thrusting you are only playing with 1/3 of the potential types of power.

If you put the three types of power together with breathing, relaxing, body alignment and Coordinated Body Motion you will have chi power.

I said this before, and repeat it so you will take note and appreciate how true and important this is.

One can honestly say that a martial art without chi power is not a true art.

And you would only be saying that a martial art that neglects putting together the basic-basics (breathing, relaxing, alignment, CBM) with sinking, rotating or thrusting is an art that is not firing on all cylinders.

APPLICATION TWENTY-ONE

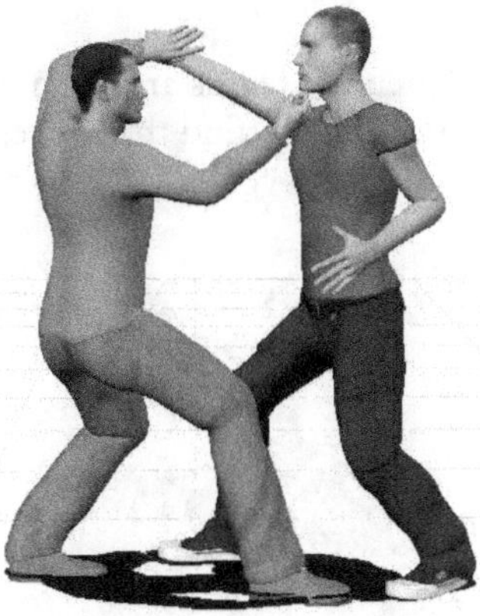

The attacker steps forward with the right foot and punches with the right hand to the face.

The defender assumes a back stance and pulls the attacker's punch upward with his left hand and executes a right punch to the chin.

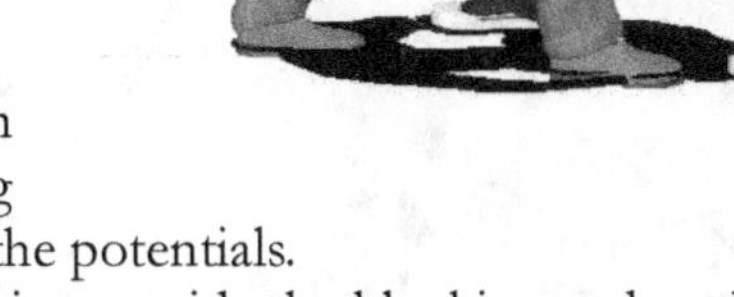

This is sort of a no brainer, and I'm somewhat surprised that I've almost never seen it. But then people get fixated on the blocking potentials and ignore the pulling the potentials.

This is what I mean by stepping outside the blocking and exploding mode and finding other energies.

Funny thing, often a different energy is nothing more than a different direction.

Note that you might need the Switch Step here, or some variation thereof.

Also, it is very easy to make this work with a slap grab, then circle the slap right back to the chin.

And, when showing this I am fond of using a finger or two. I don't strike with fingers, I place and press. Works well and the subtlety of the motion can be quite impressive. People won't feel energy coming at them, so they don't react.

When people can be knocked down, or over, or thrown, or whatever, with a simple finger or two it tends to change their minds.

NOTE

When the hands are open it is easier to translate a technique into a grab art. Can you find the moves that will allow you to change the last (mid level and high level block) into grab arts such as…

Chicken WingArmlock

Figure Four Armlock

Vertical Arm Pin

Upper Splitting

Can you make these grab arts out of other Promise Fights?

APPLICATION TWENTY-TWO

The Attacker steps forward with the right foot and punches with the right hand.

The Defender assumes a back stance as he executes an outward mid-level block and raises the right hand to the high position.

The Attacker is threatened by the Defender's right hand, and he starts to block it.

The high hand has been nothing but a distraction, however, and the Defender stabs his left hand into the Attacker's throat.

Another 'no brainer.'

The high hand is useless, held high like a threat, but actually doing nothing. Don't get distracted by threats, observe, and respond only to what is actually happening.

APPLICATION TWENTY-THREE

The Attacker steps forward with the right foot and punches with the right hand.

The Defender steps back into a back stance with the right foot as he executes a left outward mid-level block and the right hand raises to the high position.

The Defender grabs the Attacker's right wrist with his left hand and sinks back into his stance. At the same time he twists his body, uses his whole body weight, and pulls the Attacker forward and off balance.

The Defender strikes the Attacker in the face with a downward back fist, or hammer, or whatever.

So many potentials out of this mid/high blocking position, and so few people go looking.

According to Matrix Karate the mid/high position is one of the 9 arm positions which channel energy most efficiently.

Incidentally, sometimes I say 'go into a back stance,' and sometimes I say 'assume a back stance.'

To 'go into' means make it work.

'To assume' means one can use other motions (for instance: the switch step) to find the best distance.

He who controls distance controls the fight.

APPLICATION TWENTY-FOUR

The Attacker steps forward with the right foot and punches with the right hand.

The Defender simultaneously executes a left outer mid-level block and a left front snap kick.

I call this technique 'stop-kick,' because you are stopping the attacker with a kick.

The trick is to kick him before his rear foot passes his front foot, as this is when he is going 'uphill.'

Once his rear foot passes his front foot he is going 'downhill,' and his weight will be more difficult to stop with a kick.

You can block and kick, or, as in the image above, you can grab and kick.

It's okay to separate these two techniques and show the blocking version to beginners, and grab and pull with intermediate students.

A good follow up technique would be for the defender to execute a right reverse punch.

The real key to a stop kick technique is to sense that the opponent is going to strike before he strikes. This depends upon the student's ability to put aside aggression, and to do the technique with a calm state of mind.

Go back through your techniques and see which ones you can do and see what is happening before the attacker does it.

Eventually, using this method, even the most uncoordinated student will see the future and be able to handle attacks

A wonderful combat technique is to stick the left hand out, and when the defender blocks it you snap that kick in.

I used to do thousands of kicks a day, trying to make my feet fast enough to do this. Looking back, I wish I had done tens of thousands of kicks.

APPLICATION TWENTY-FIVE

This is not so much a Promise Fight as a combat application.

If a person grabs you, in life or freestyle, his hand(s) are busy, so you use your feet.

Use the 'stomping/ supercharging' part of Chiang Nan Two. Keep your balance, pump your support leg up and down, and snap your foot out.

Even if the fellow has caught your foot and is holding it, this technique can work.

The key, of course, is to center your tan tien, to align your body, whether pushing or pulling, punching or kicking, so that the energy goes to and from the tan tien.

If you pull, turn your hips so your whole body weight is behind the pull.

Set up a two man exercise:

Face your partner in horse stances. Partner A leans and strikes with the front hand for the face. Partner B blocks and grabs, and counters with a side kick.

Or, do the 'Plant and push:' one same horse stances, place your foot on your partner's waist (belt) and push. This will build up tremendous leg strength that is perfect for the side kick.

Another drill is to have one fellow grabs your arm, and you stomp and pull and kick. Have him 'drive' you around the room, and learn to work this technique from any position.

After you have done a couple of minutes, then change and you do the holding while he learns to supercharge and kick and pulls and so on.

A NOTE

The next move in this form is after the kick, it is a 180 turn of the body as you stomp the foot and face the other direction.

This move trains you to fight in two directions.

However, you should avoid this situation and learn to apply the following strategy.

To fight two people you create a sandwich, with you one of the outside pieces of bread, and one of the attackers as the meat. That way they have to get past one another, and you only fight one person.

To fight two people is to split your intention.

So to fight two people is a matter of strategy, not technique.

Always avoid being the meat, with the attacker's as the bread on either side.

Always be on the outside, with them getting in each other's way.

A wonderful drill for this is 'two on one rhythmic freestyle.'

Attacker one strikes, defender blocks and counters.
Attacker two strikes, defender blocks and counters.
Attacker one strikes, defender blocks and counters.
Attacker two strikes, defender blocks and counters.
And so on.

Participants in the drill may only take one step when they block, and one step when they strike.

The drill is done slowly. The purpose is not to beat the man in the center up, but to teach him how to fight, how to strategize and keep opponents where he wants them.

APPLICATION TWENTY-SIX

The attacker steps forward with the left foot and punches with the left hand.

The defender steps back with the right foot and slaps the attacker's hand past with a right palm.

The attacker punches with the right hand.

The defender pivots to the right as he executes a single left knife hand block.

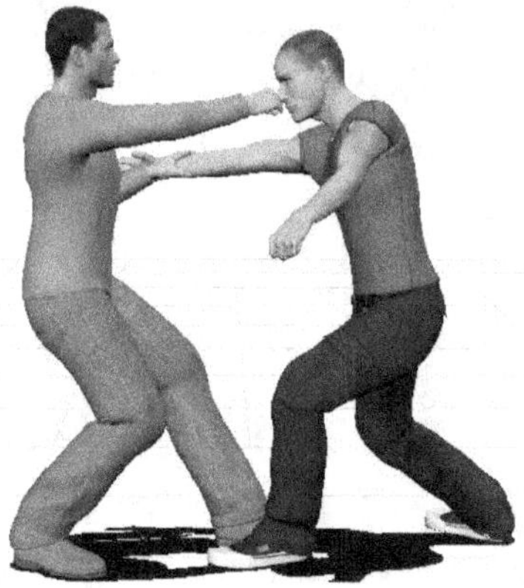

The defender grabs the attacker's right wrist with his left hand and pivots to the left, pulling the attacker in to a right punch.

If pulling is not an option, the defender can simply shuffle forward to execute his right punch to the face.

A NOTE

Many people dismiss the knife hand block, call it classical folderol that doesn't work in a real fight.

But it would be easier to teach a child a knife hand block, and ignore the 'slap/grab' potential, which is likely what the Okinawans did when they translated the pinans into forms for school children around 1905.

But, as I stated earlier, the slap/grab is heart of the art, it happens first, then the grab, then the block.

So if you revert from the single knife to the 'slap/grab' technique, there is a complete art that can be matrixed out of this one technique. An art that is more than combat ready. It is close in, presents all kinds of weapons, and can be used to throw the opponent around quite easily.

Consider the following matrixing data.

To push the hand across the body is to 'close' it.
To push the hand outward, exposing the body, is to 'open it.
Thus, you have four potential slap/grab techniques

close/close
close/open
open/close
close/close

Explore how you would use these four potentials with the slap/grab presented in the simple single knife hand block.

APPLICATION TWENTY-SEVEN

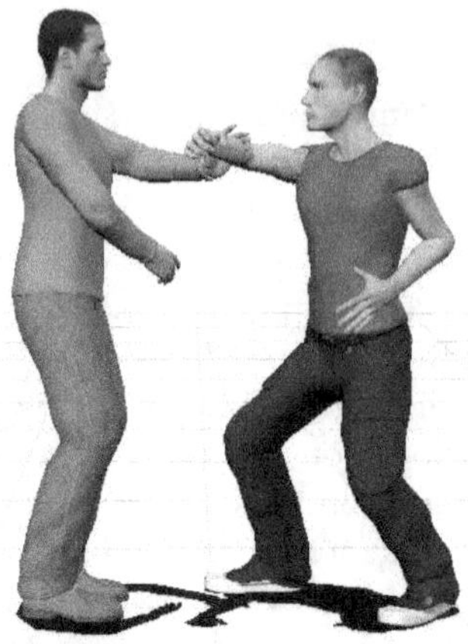

The attacker steps forward with the right foot and punches to the face with the right hand.

The defender slaps the right hand past with his left palm.

He might step back, or just lean back, to do this.

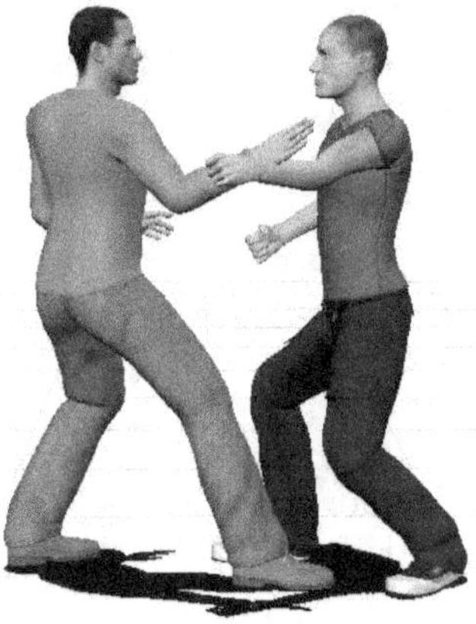

The attacker punches with the left hand.

The defender steps forward with the right foot into a back stance as he executes a right single knife hand block.

The defender strikes the side of the attacker's neck with a 'reverse hammer fist with a thumb extended.'

That is, he strikes him in the neck with the thumb.

But, we don't have to end here.

The defender grabs the attacker's neck (or shoulder, or jacket or whatever), and now the fun starts.

The defender can pull the attacker forward as he executes a right knee to the groin, a left elbow strike (into grab art) and so on.

Or, if the attacker isn't set up quite right, there is one of my favorites, a good, old sweep!

Kick, punch, knee, elbow, sweep, throw one way or another with whatever body part comes to hand…there is no end to the potentials once a Karateka has managed to put his hands on an attacker.

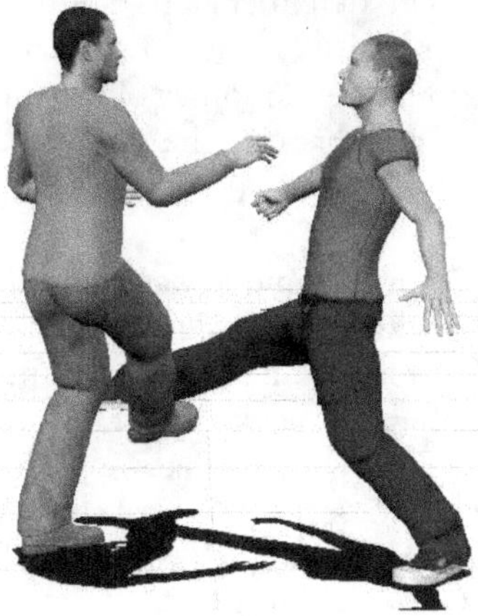

APPLICATION TWENTY-EIGHT

The attacker steps forward with the right foot and punches with the right hand.

The defender steps back with the right foot into a back stance as he executes a double knife hand block.

The attacker punches with the left hand.

The defender steps/shifts forward into a front stance as he executes a left smother block and a right spear hand to the throat.

This technique was originally done with a vertical spear hand. But the horizontal spearhead fits into the neck cavity better.

Which means that we will have to look for a vertical spear hand application, which we will find on the next page.

APPLICATION TWENTY-NINE

The attacker steps forward with the right foot and punches with the right hand.

The defender steps forward with the left foot into a front stance as he executes a smother block and shoots the right hand (vertical spear) past the attacker's neck.

The defender pushes down and into a circle with his left arm, pushing the attacker's arm up around behind him. At t5he same time he pushes down and to the right on the neck with his right hand.

This is called a 'rotary throw' in Aikido, but it is plain to see that it was hidden inside the karate moves, too.

I call it an 'insertion throw,' because we are inserting the hand past the body.

You can also insert the spear hand on the other side of the neck, under the arms, between the legs, and so on.

The defender should learn how to do a shoulder roll out of the technique.

You can also do this throw out of a knife hand block.

APPLICATION THIRTY

The Attacker steps forward with the right foot and punches with the right hand.

The defender steps back with the left foot into a back stance as he executes a right slap with the palm.

The Defender executes a left grab.

The right hand prepares for the knife hand block.

The defender pulls the attacker's right hand and executes a knife hand block (chop) to the side of the attacker's neck.

This is the classic 'slap/grab/ technique. You can do it with other strikes, a kick or an elbow, whatever.

The defender extends the right arm, making the block/chop into an insertion technique.

The defender pushes down and to the right with his right hand, and pushes the attacker's right arm up and around.

The defender should step forward with the left leg and pivot as he does the technique.

NOTES

This is a sort of a variation on the Rotary Throw. I call it the Vertical arm pin because the attacker's arm should be vertical to the ground.

It is not as easy to roll out of, and the defender should learn how to take the attacker down and lock the attacker on the ground.

You might need to use the switch step in this technique, but it is better if you learn it so well you can make your step and motion simply circular.

In an insertion throw you don't just make the arm straight and stiff, you point in a direction forever. It will work best when you actually forget about the opponent, point forever, and draw circles with your finger on the cosmos.

APPLICATION THIRTY-ONE

The attacker steps forward with the right foot and punches with the right hand.

The defender steps back with the right foot into a back stance as he executes a knife hand block.

The attacker punches with the left hand.

The defender pulls the left foot back and twists to the left, executing a right outward block.

The defender grabs/pulls the attackers' left hand as he executes a right front snap to the groin.

Alternate targets are the belly (preferred) or the thigh of the back leg just under the testicles.

The defender sets his foot down in a front stance as he executes a left punch.

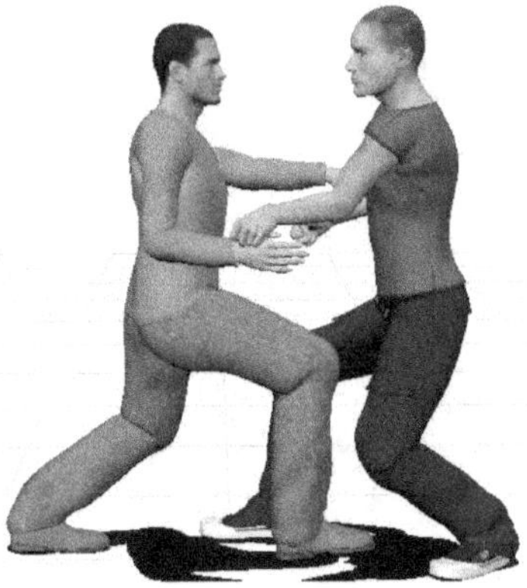

APPLICATION THIRTY-TWO

The attacker steps forward with the right foot as he punches with the right hand.

The defender steps forward with the left foot into a front stance as he executes a left outward block.

The defender pulls the attacker's right arm with his left hand as he punches with his right hand.

CONCLUSION TO THE PROMISE FIGHTS OF CHIANG NAN TWO

During the course of the promise fights of this form the defender has deliberately charged the attacker.

In the beginning the defender always steps back, learns to harmonize the motion of the bodies, keep the distance set, has time to build his defense.

When charging the technique the defender is saying 'I don't have to react, I can act!' In other words, he is not victim to time, but in charge of time.

The sequence of timing goes like this.

white belt	see/think/react
green belt	see/react
brown belt	react
black belt	act

The good martial artist sees what is coming before it comes. This is easily done if he practices a good system…a matrixed system.

Chapter Five
Chiang Nan Three

Below are the videos for form Three.

channan 3 ~ https://youtu.be/VTzych_8GDQ	1:21
channan 3 side ~ https://youtu.be/Ztv_EPF5vvE	1:23
channan 3 explained ~ https://youtu.be/yr7iaOx1OXc	3:52
channan 3 app 16 ~ https://youtu.be/yIF5qNylY-c	8:16
channan 3 app 17 ~ https://youtu.be/aDwRclDzbhA	4:42
channan 3 app 18 ~ https://youtu.be/1TmVCsfVRZg	5:11
channan 3 app 19 ~ https://youtu.be/kh69nrOGnzc	8:16
channan 3 app 20 ~ https://youtu.be/C6fBTlXfLCQ	4:34
channan 3 app 21 ~ https://youtu.be/1Oq_iylI4L4	12:57
	43:16

Chiang Nan Three

One of the biggest influences on Karate was kung fu.

The arts that came to Okinawa came from all over the orient, but the main influx came directly from China.

Whether it was shipwrecked sailers, priests in a foreign land, ambassadors, fighting men trading techniques, or whatever, China just seemed to have a better relationship with Okinawa.

I have written before about the various types of Kung Fu that came to Okinawa, and specifically of Pan Gai Noon.

Pan Gai Noon was a unique lineage imported by Kanbun Uechi. It was very powerful, and this art was where I stumbled over the 'slap/grab' concept. Where I deleted others concepts and began to focus on the slap grab which is inherent in the Uechi technique called 'wa uke,' which means, I believe, 'circular block.'

Circular block, yet it was being used hard style.

Why not soft?

Why not circular, as the name states?

And, as I began to examine the various kung fu systems I saw a vast study of circularity in the arts. Be it Shaolin or Praying Mantis, or whatever, circularity seemed to rule the day.

Unfortunately, the circles seemed…large.

But this may just be a teaching device. Give the student a large circle so he can see it, then help him make it smaller and smaller.

Maybe the Okinawans were teaching circularity in just the hips, which tends to obscure it to the beginner who has never seen the larger circles.

At any rate, after I had examined Pan Gai Noon to a great extent, which examinations are available in my book by that name, I began to explore slap/grab in the classical karate arts not related to Uechi ryu.

My original art was Kang Duk Won, and I was quite aware of the small circle of the hips inherent in virtually every move, but that was limited to concepts of more linear explosions. It took almost nothing for me to understand how to make bigger circles with the hips and the arms. But this slap/grab thing…that was something else.

So, having studied Northern Shaolin Ton Toi, and Southern Shaolin Fut Ga, I let the circles of the techniques occur, which they do naturally if you just 'go with the flow,' and looked for places to substitute slap/grab for the hard fist.

To be honest, there were many things I didn't like. Things which made me understand why the circles were somewhat deleted and became 'secrets.'

A lot of this had to do with teaching children.

A child just does not understand subtlety.

A child grasps a hard block ten times easier than a subtle shift of the hips, a slap and a grab.

Which made me rethink why the Okinawans 'dumbed down' their karate for school children.

It was just easier to make kids bash arms than teach them how to manipulate flows.

And it wasn't all laziness; I have a pure system in the Kang Duk Won, and I have encountered the same frustrations in teaching that, doubtless, the Okinawan Masters experienced when they translated Karate into something that could be taught to young bodies and minds.

CHIANG NAN THREE

Stand in a natural stance.

Pivot to the left into a back stance (hips squared) as you guard the face with a right palm block. The left hand should scoop across the mid-section in preparation for a knife hand block.

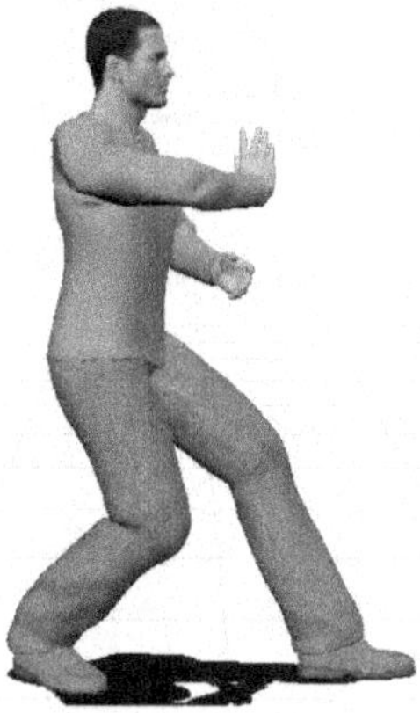

Pivot the hips back to the right and align the body as you execute a right knife hand block.

This is actually a 'slap/grab' movement.

Bring the right foot up to the left foo and lean at the ankles as you execute a left low block and a right mid-level block.

Step forward with the left foot, traveling through a back stance, as you guard the face with a left palm.

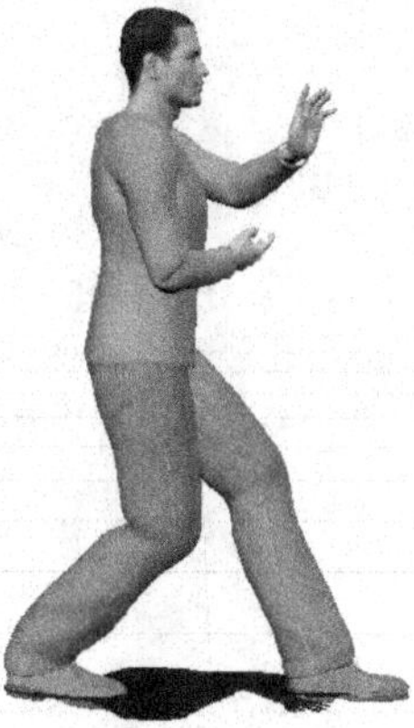

Pivot to the right into a horse stance as you execute a right high block and a left chop.

Pivot to the right 180 degrees. Move the right hand in an outward circle and bring the left hand across the body.

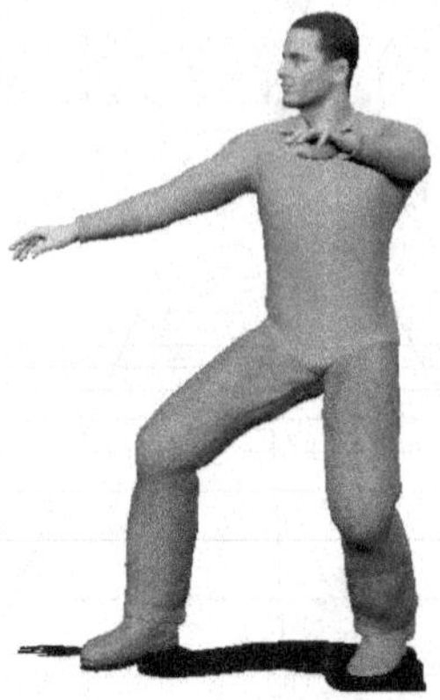

Assume a back stance (hips squared) with the right foot forward as you execute a left palm block. The right hand should scoop across the mid-section in preparation for a knife hand block.

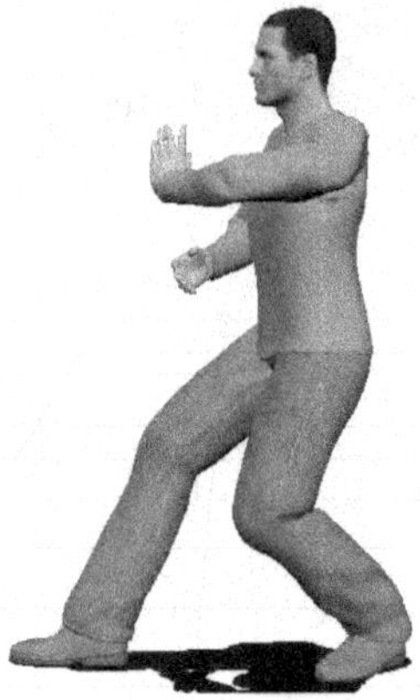

Turn the hips to the left to align the body as you execute a single knife hand block.

Bring the left foot up next to the right foot and lean at the ankles as you execute a left outward middle block and a right low block.

Step forward with the right foot (traveling through a back stance) as you guard the face with the right palm.

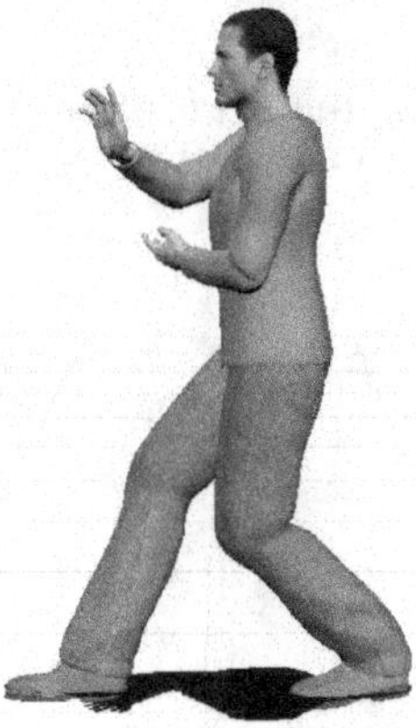

Pivot to the left into a horse stance as you execute a left high block and a right chop.

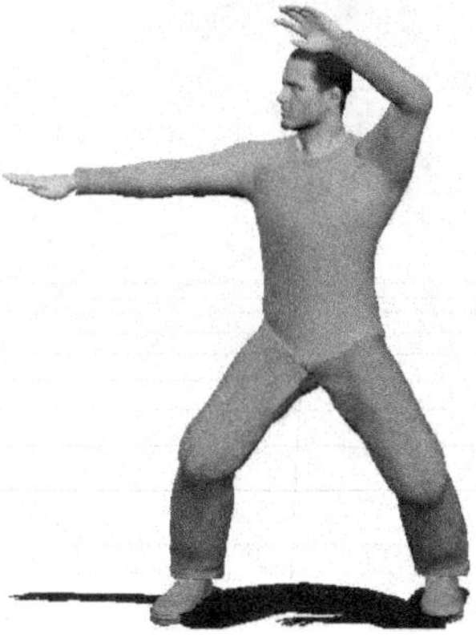

Bring the right foot forward and turn 90 degrees to the left as you guard the face with the right palm and protect the body with an inverted low block (reverse parry).

Extend the left foot into a back stance as you execute a left outward grabbing block.

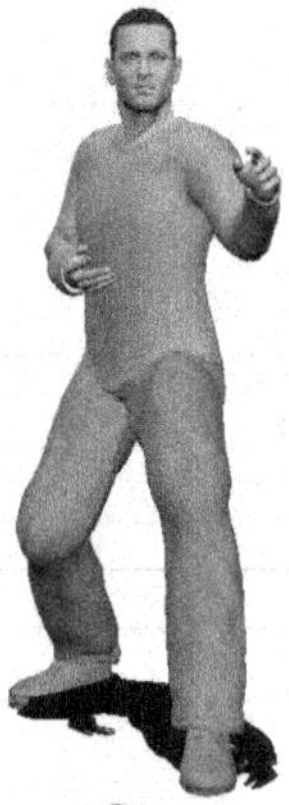

Bring the left foot back in a switch step. Circle the left hand inward to execute a low block.

Step forward with the right foot into a front stance as you execute a right spear under a left palm.

Circle the right hand inward and the left hand outward as you step behind the right foot with the left foot (cross stance)

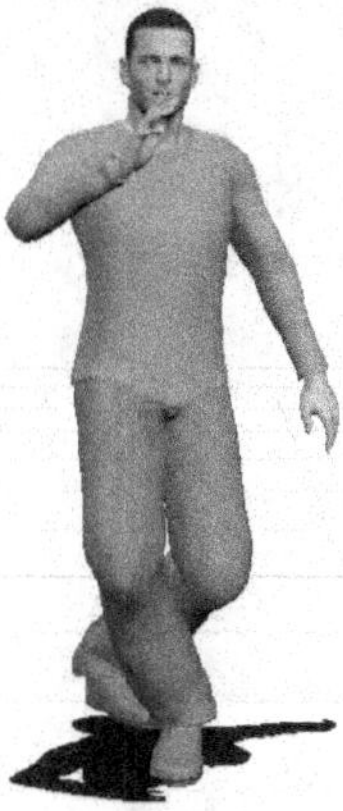

Pivot to the right as you step to the rear with the right foot into a crossed kneeling stance.

The arms should continue to circle into a left palm block and a right vertical hammer fist (to the groin).

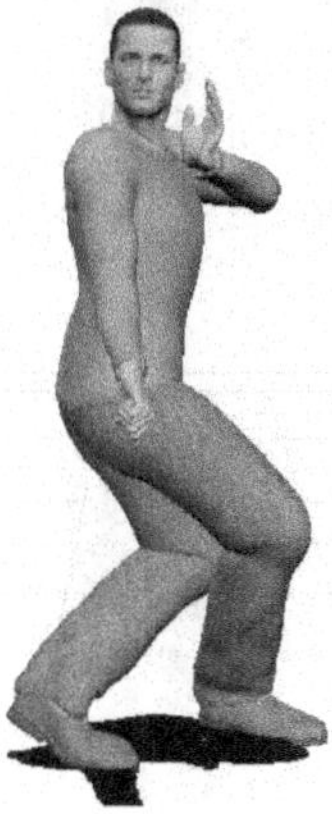

Pivot in place (left) into a horse stance as you execute a right high block and a left chop.

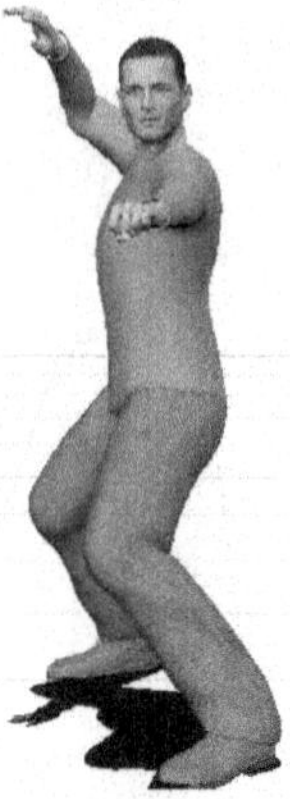

Bring the left foot back as you circle the left hand outward.

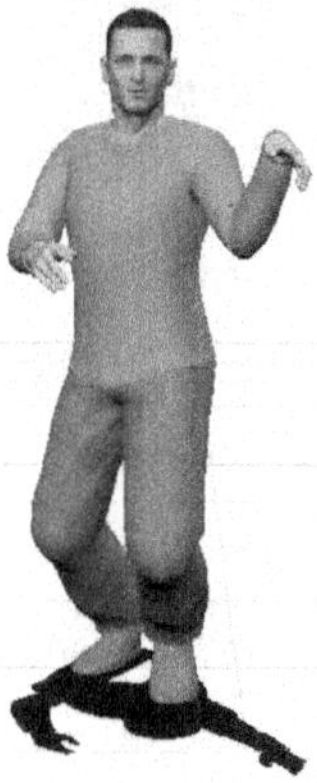

Step forward with the right foot into a front stance as you execute a right punch.

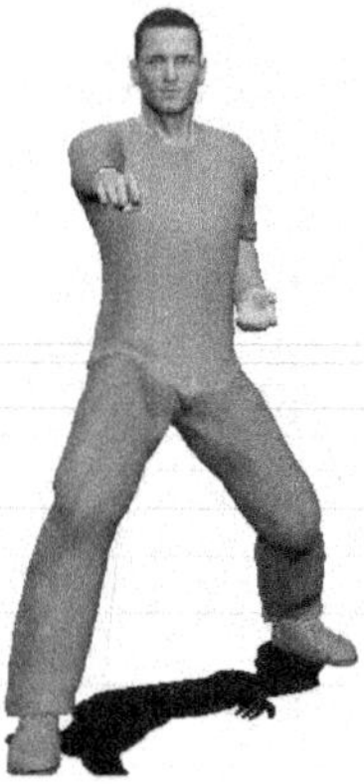

Bring the left foot behind the right foot, touching the left toe to the right heel.

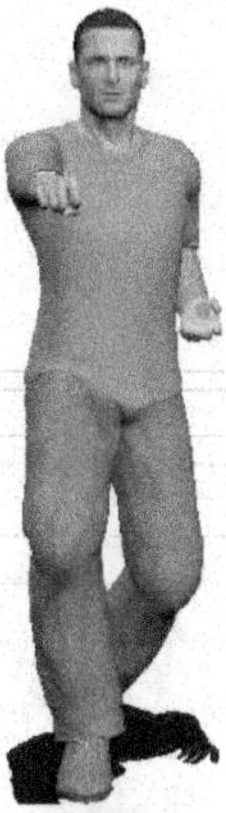

Pivot to the right 180 degrees. Pivot on the left ball of the foot and the right heel so the feet end up next to each other.

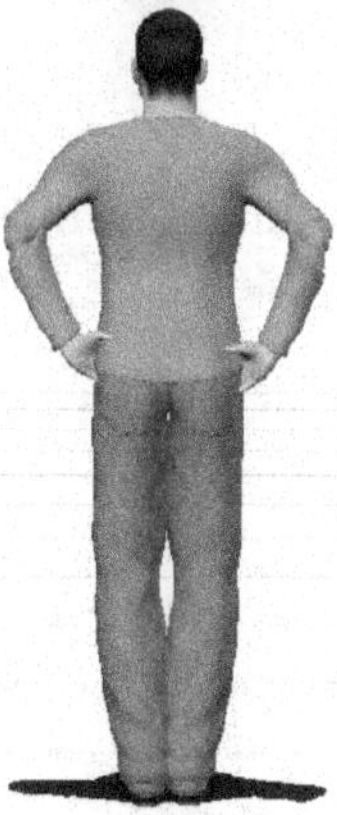

Begin to bend the knees as you cross and scoop the arms in front of you.

Side view of last move.

Bring the hands up ward as you bend the knees further.

Side view of the last move.

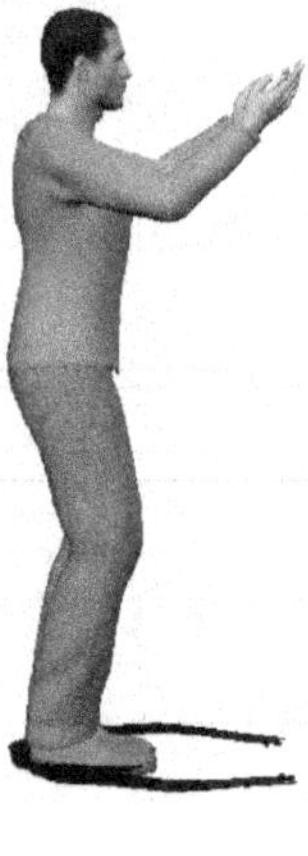

Bend the knees more as you overturn the hands into double outward grabbing blocks.

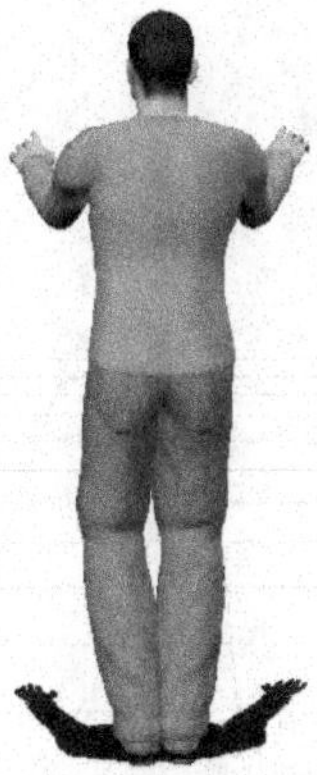

Side view of last move.

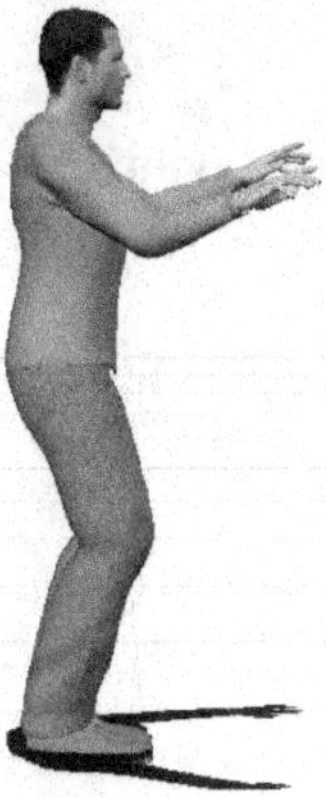

Execute a right leg raise.

Side view of last move.

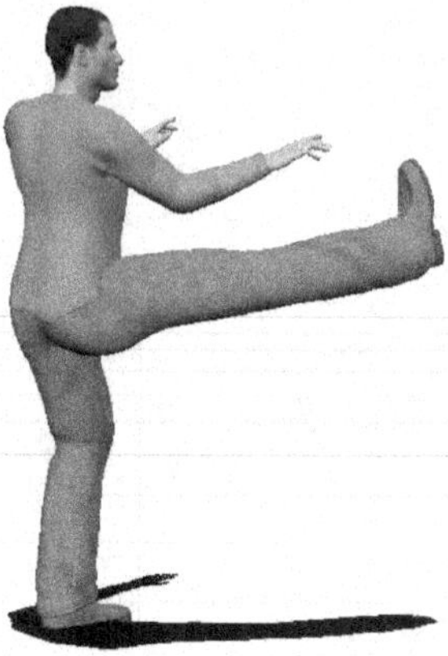

Set the right foot down as you lower the arms.

Pivot into a horse stance, placing the hands on the waist, as you execute a right elbow block.

The hands should be placed on the waist.

The right shoulder should be slightly turned into the block.

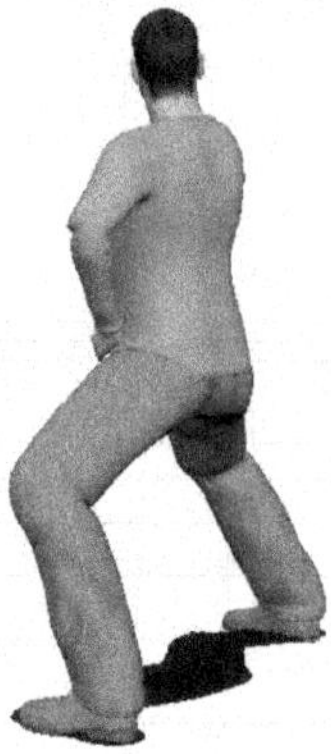

Side view of the last move.

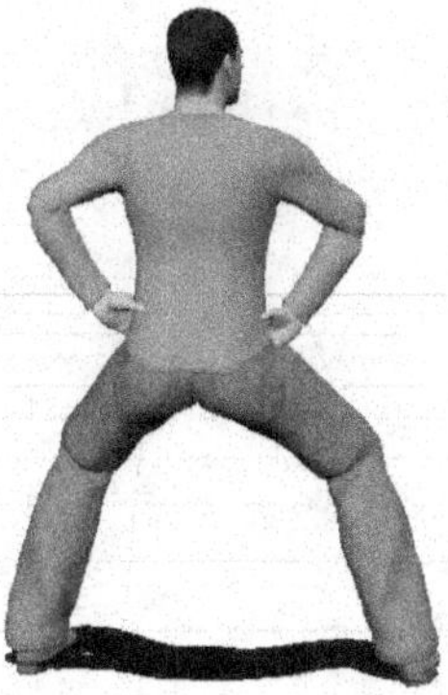

Execute a right snapping back hand.

Originally this was a fist, but closing the fist locks up energy, an open hand, in the end, is faster.

Empty the mind to empty the body, then you will achieve speed.

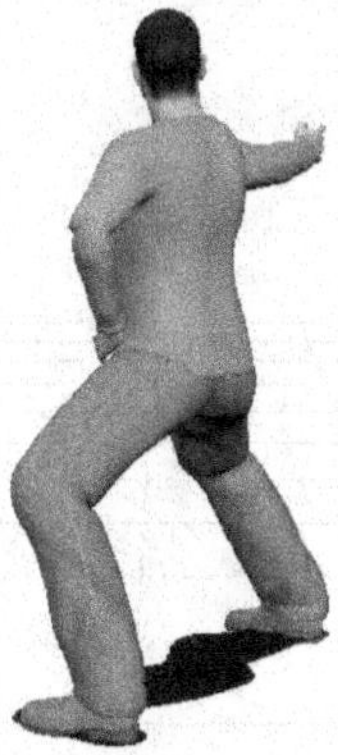

Side view of the last move.

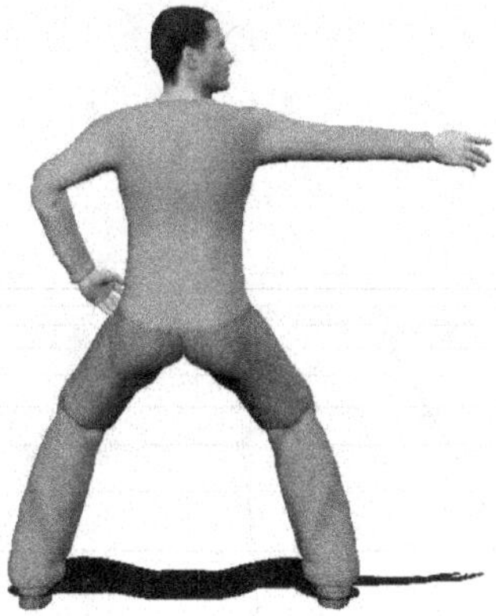

Bring the elbow back to the original position (hand on waist).

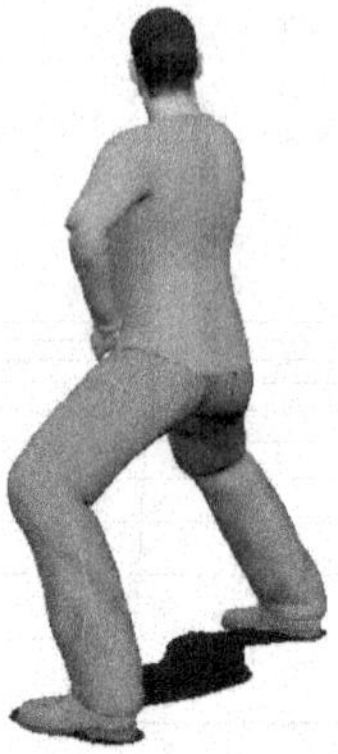

Bring the right foot back to a cat stance (switch step) as you cross the hands low and circle them outward to double outward grabbing blocks.

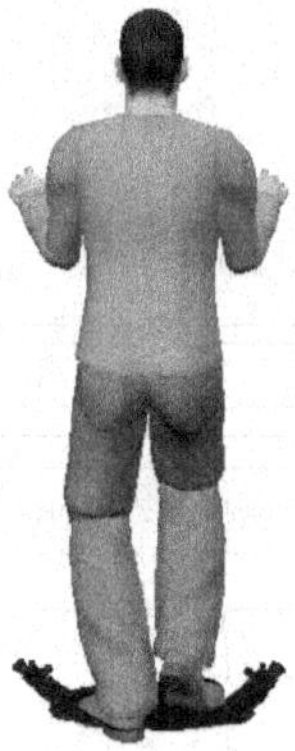

Execute a left leg raise.

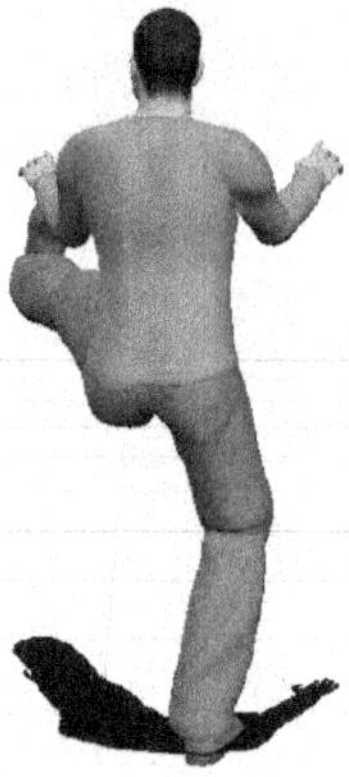

Lower the left foot as you bring the arms down.

Pivot to the right into a horse stance, placing the hands on the waist, as you execute a left elbow block.

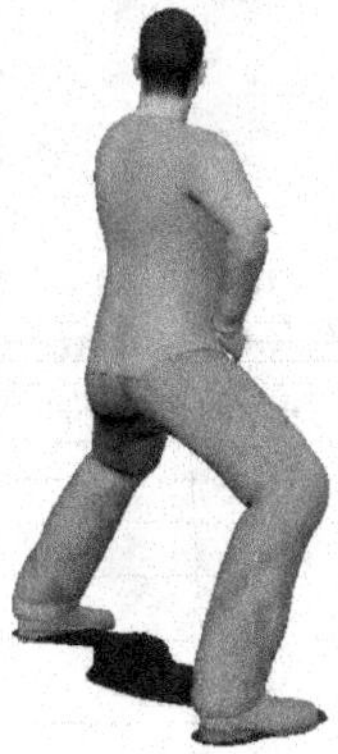

Execute a left snapping back hand.

Don't think muscle, rather visualize where you want your back hand to go, and let it go.

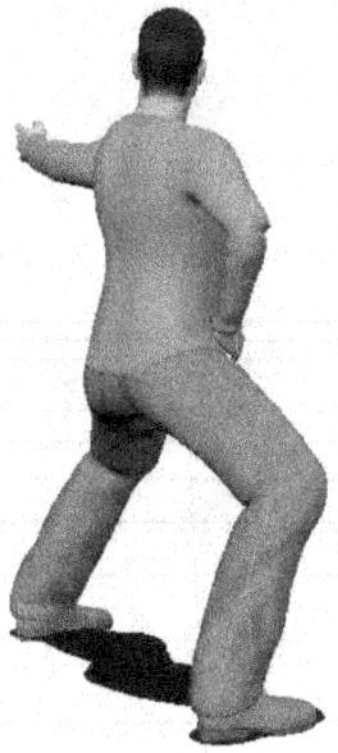

Return the left arm to the blocking elbow position.

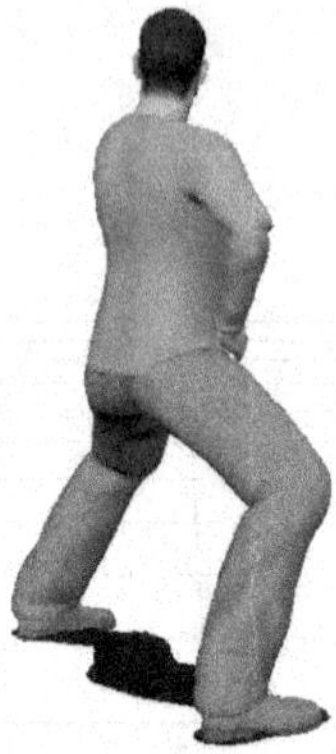

Bring the left foot back to a cat stance (switch stance) as you circle the hands across the lower body, then raise them in outward circles to outward grabbing blocks.

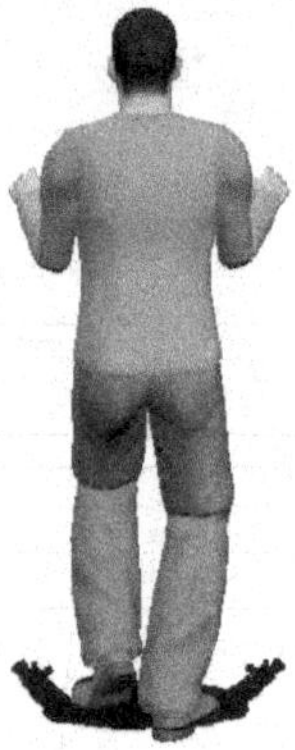

Execute a right leg raise.

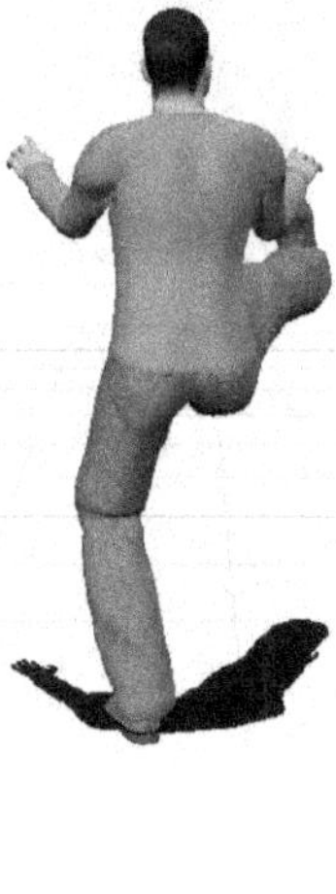

Lower the right foot and pivot into a horse stance as you execute a right elbow block.

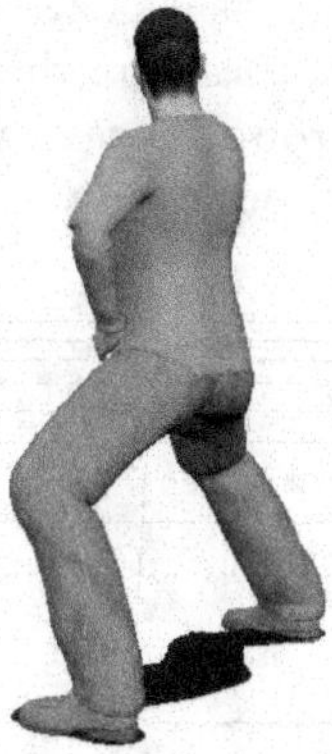

Execute a right snapping back hand.

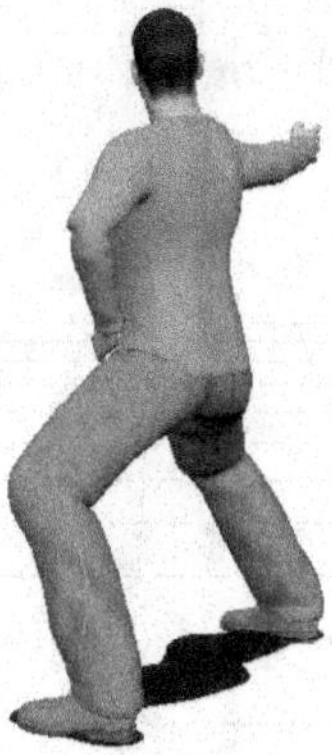

Bring the right foot back to the cat stance (switch step) as you circle the right hand outward.

Step forward with the left foot into a front stance as you execute a left punch.

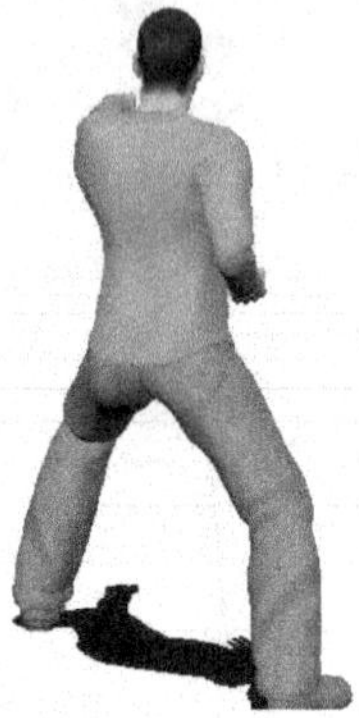

Bring the right foot forward.

Step to the right, behind the right foot, with the left foot (180 degrees) into a horse stance as you execute aright two finger strike.

Execute a left two finger strike.

Execute a right spear hand over the left shoulder and a left elbow to the rear.

Execute a left two finger strike.

Execute a right two finger strike.

Execute a left spear hand over the right shoulder and a left elbow strike to the rear.

Return to the natural position.

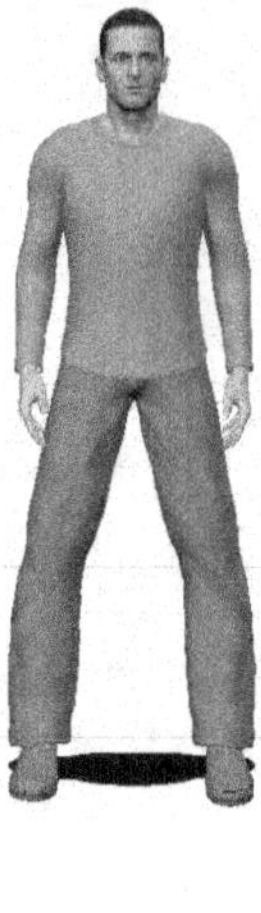

CHIANG NAN THREE

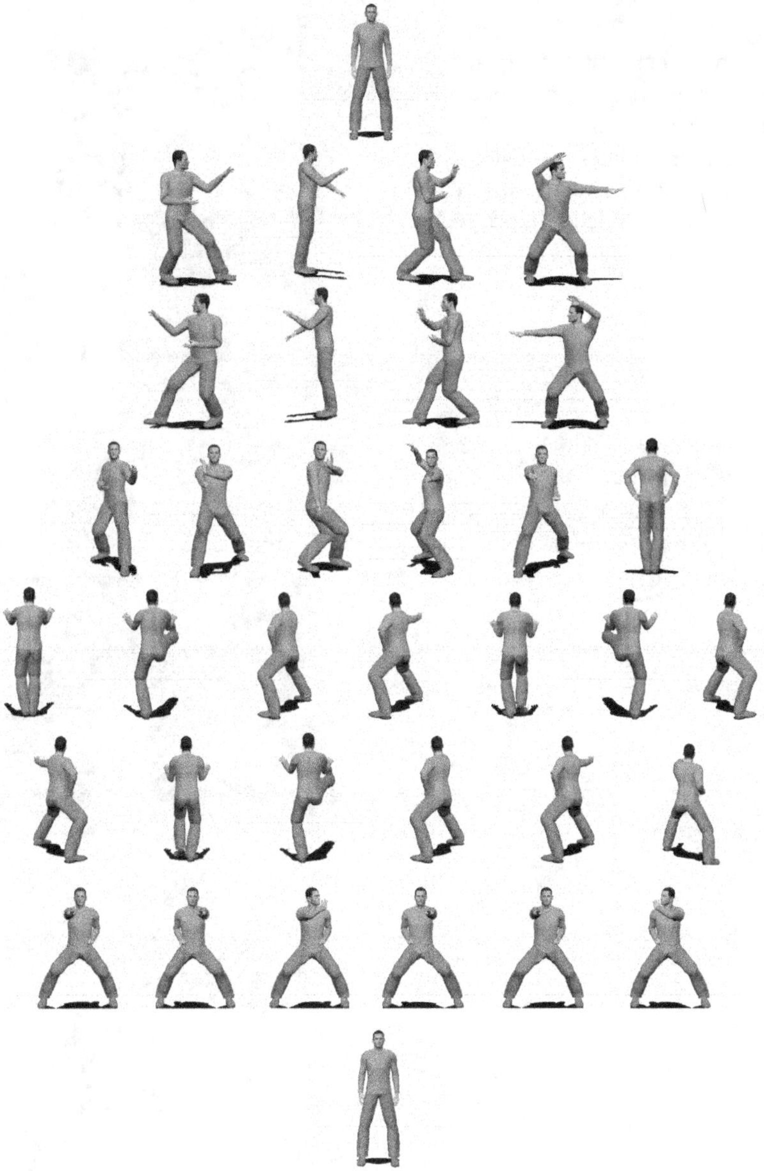

APPLICATION THIRTY-THREE

The attacker steps forward with the right hand and punches with the right hand.

The defender steps back with the right foot into a back stance as he executes a left knife hand (palm stop).

The attacker punches with the left hand.

The defender begins to pivot to the right as he moves forward with the left foot and executes a left palm block.

The defender sinks into a horse stance as he translates the left palm into a right grab and executes a left hammer fist to the torso.

One could add a right pubic punch at this point, and collapse the attacker to the ground.

APPLICATION THIRTY-FOUR

The attacker steps forward with the right foot and punches with the right hand.

The defender steps back with his right foot into a back stance and executes a left knife hand (palm stop).

The attacker punches with the left hand.

The defender steps back with the left foot and stands up and leans forward as he parries the punch past his belly with a left parry.

Note: the technique could end here with a finger poke to the eye. But we wouldn't be so cruel. He he.

The attacker punches to the face with the right hand.

The defender leans back slightly and executes a left palm. The right hand is preparing to execute its part of the 'slap/grab.'

The defender steps forward with the left foot into a horse state behind the attacker's right foot.

He traps the attacker's right arm a right hook, extends his left hand across the throat, and executes a 'splitting' throw.

Splitting is when the lower part of the body goes one way, and the upper part of the body goes the other way.

This technique was originally a middle/low block, followed by another middle/low block, which is often translated as an arm twine (crossing the opponents arms and using one as a lever to execute an elbow lock/throw.

This is fine, but it is difficult, and snapping the fists closed in the blocks tends to slow down the ability of the hands to catch and manipulate to a twine.

With the open hands of slap/grab the flow of the hands is uninterrupted by closing the fists.

And, by using just one slap/grab to enter the technique we make it much more combat effective.

On note: karate is often developed solely for defense against a straight punch. But the world knows boxing, and the hook punch, so we have to adapt and be wary when applying our techniques. The slap/grab is very amenable to force or flow, as in stopping a punch by palming the biceps, or slipping the punch with a parry or slap.

Incidentally, if one is not close enough to split, they can always utilize an elbow spike to the body.

APPLICATION THIRTY-FIVE

The attacker steps forward with the right foot as he punches with the right hand.

The defender steps forward with the right foot into a front stance as he executes a left palm block and a right spear to the throat.

The technique could end here, except that it is unrealistic. After all, what is to stop the attacker from smothering the spear strike by simply pushing down with his right hand? Doesn't the palm block actually create a defense for the defensive technique?

So, this is not the real technique. The real technique is not done with a rigid stance and strike and block. The real technique is to throw a hook punch, right over the attacker's hook punch, catch the attacker's fist with the left palm, and point the right finger at the ground.

Pointing directly at one's own foot foot cause an 'inversion' of the attacker's elbow. It is VERY simple to just lower the attacker to the ground by lowering your stance.

A note: I often point when doing techniques. This is how I direct intention. Your intention is how you direct chi power; the pointing finger tells your power where to go.

Point as if forever. Forget about the body resisting you and point. Your techniques will become wondrous, simple, and take no effort.

APPLICATION THIRTY-SIX

The attacker steps forward with the right foot and punches with the right hand.

The defender steps forward and inward with his right foot, nudging his toes against the attacker's right foot.

Simultaneously he uses a right palm to slap the attacker's punch outward. The left hand is going under for the grab.

The defender grabs the attackers right hand with his left hand and executes a right hammer to the groin.

The defender is beginning to spin.

The defender brings the right arm up to secure the attacker's right arm, pivots into a horse stance, and throws the attacker by levering the right arm across his shoulder.

The defender should be careful of the attacker's left hand when spinning into the technique.

I always hold my laughter when people say karate has no throws.

APPLICATION THIRTY-SEVEN

The attacker steps forward with the right foot and punches with the right hand.

The defender steps forward and inward with the right foot, pointing the toes towards the attacker's foot.

The defender steps behind himself with the left foot, spins, and executes a left elbow to the attacker's face.

If the defender can't keep spinning he can do several things, a left backwards sweep with the right leg, enough of a turn to deliver a right punch, etc.

If the defender can keep spinning, and can get behind the attacker, he can grab the shoulders, or the head, keep spinning, and throw the attacker to the ground.

If he is close enough, and wishes to, he can apply a choke of some sort.

A rigid, set in stone technique cannot adapt to the vagaries of real combat, so your techniques must have options, you must be flexible, you must be liquid in your approach to combat.

APPLICATION THIRTY-EIGHT

The attacker steps forward with the left foot and pushes the shoulders.

The defender steps back with the left foot and brings his hands up the center, then executes double outward grabbing blocks.

The defender pivots to the right, pulling the attacker's left arm with his right hand and executing a left elbow strike to the face.

The defender straightens his left arm and steps forward with his right foot. He pushes down on the attacker's neck with his left arm and pushes the attacker's left arm up and around.

This will result in an earlier technique called a Vertical Arm Pin.

Most people, when they push, or punch, for that matter, are overbalancing themselves to the front. This makes it very easy to do simple techniques like the elbow strike. Once the attacker is dazed it is easy to manipulate and throw him. This technique, of striking to daze and then manipulating, is called 'Shock and Lock.'

APPLICATION THIRTY-NINE

The attacker step forward with the left foot to punch the defender.

The defender moves in front of the attack and executes a left leg raise to the groin.

The attacker is slightly bent over (or not) and decides to execute a left punch anyway.

The defender sets his foot down and pivots into a horse stance as he executes a left elbow block.

The defender snaps a backlist to the body.

A back fist is not designed for power, it is best utilized with snap. But the technique must be practiced until it is faster than a magician dealing cards, faster than the attacker can prepare for it.

A wonderful, little addition to this technique, is the 'tripping the tiger' technique from Monkey Boxing.

The defender shuffles forward, throwing the attacker's arm up and ducking past it.

This is a simple technique, but very subtle, and sometimes difficult for students to do.

Students always think they have to lift the rear heel to make the technique work, but lifting the heel shows they don't understand the technique.

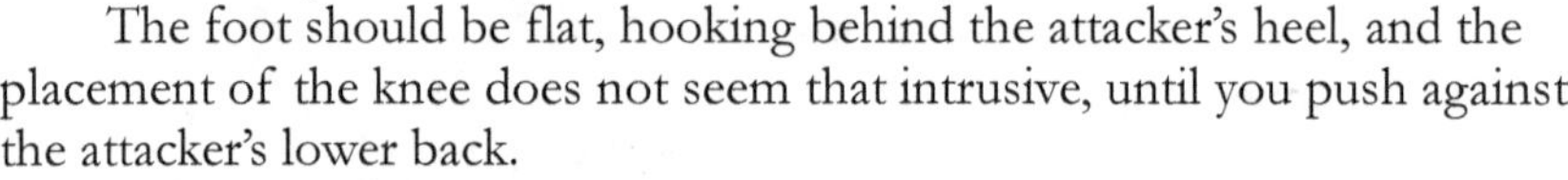

The foot should be flat, hooking behind the attacker's heel, and the placement of the knee does not seem that intrusive, until you push against the attacker's lower back.

This is a 'splitting technique.'

APPLICATION FORTY

The attacker attempts a bearhug trapping the arms.

The defender steps to the side in a horse stance as he thrusts both hands to the front.

This puts his whole weight on the attacker's grab, which will unbalance him.

This also sinks a ground, making the defender very firm in his position.

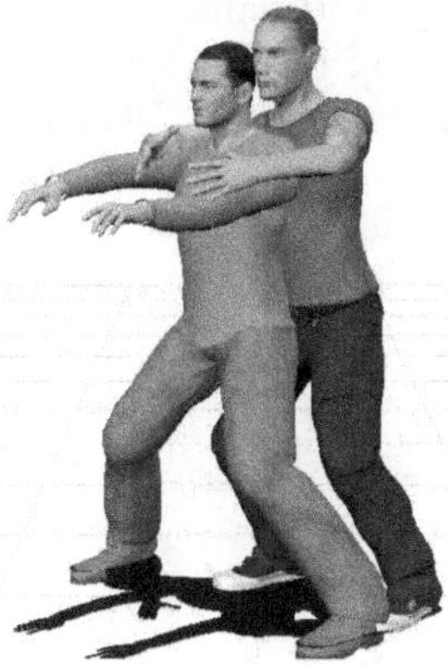

The defender executes a left elbow spike to the midsection and a right spear thrust to the eyes.

There are actually a lot of things you can do when a bearhug is attempted.

Stomp the instep, grab the groin, manipulate the fingers, and so on.

The fact of the matter, however, is that you should feel the attack coming, and move in front of it.

On the next page is one of the techniques that was hidden, has not been too well known, outside of some good judo or jujitsu.

The defender grabs the right arm and kneels, pivoting to the left as he does so.

The arm is the lever for a wonderful over the shoulder throw.

NOTE

You will notice that some techniques have many options. A rigid, set in stone technique cannot adapt to the vagaries of real combat, so your techniques must have options, you must be flexible, you must be liquid in your approach to combat. Practice your techniques with great focus, understand they are a template, but know that the template must sometimes be bent to accommodate reality.

CONCLUSION TO THE PROMISE FIGHTS OF CHAING NAN THREE

As stated, if you let the attack reach you, you have already messed up.

As a student you should not be looking at the body, or anticipating the 'pre-set' attack, you should be watching the attacker's intention, moving with him, getting in front of the technique.

This takes much practice, but is the point of the martial arts.

Learn to see what an attacker is going to do before he does it.

Don't 'react,' for 're-' mean after, and that means you are moving after the attack, when it is to late.

Instead, act.

This what it means to be 'in the now.'

Unfortunately, so many people think this is to be aggressive, to hit first, which is to be the bully.

The real martial artist doesn't move first aggressively, he moves with, in concert with, using as little force as necessary.

This is not emotion…meaning anger, or some other emotional harmonic, this is putting aside emotion so you can see reality as it is.

Never let yourself be reduced to fighting, to making the art and discipline of the martial arts into a sport.

A sport is contending with an opponent.

In an art the opponent is your mind, your emotions, anything that distracts you from finding your true spirit.

Yes, you will go through a certain amount of fighting, but the point should not be to have the joy of combat, but to reduce emotion to a calmness that will serve you no matter how frantic the chaos.

Chapter Six
Chiang Nan Four

Below are the videos for form Four.

channan 4 ~ https://youtu.be/g4Ots202ssM	1:21
channan 4 side ~ https://youtu.be/tX2MJPd1KFU	1:26
channan 4 explain ~ https://youtu.be/ebpclZmgxxQ	4:08
channan 4 app 33 ~ https://youtu.be/NDsA6g3b2dY	2:22
channan 4 app 34 ~ https://youtu.be/RCXEuAqH4sc	6:19
channan 4 app 35 ~ https://youtu.be/FXGgL9bkSmw	8:26
channan 4 app 36 ~ https://youtu.be/y7FQDxE3pjk	6:43
channan 4 app 37 ~ https://youtu.be/fwsd2OP1P9U	7:55
channan 4 app 38 ~ https://youtu.be/nOi4sDrC1N8	5:32
channan 4 app 39 ~ https://youtu.be/iDsVi_PSPEg	7:00
	44:47

Chiang Nan Four

One thing I noticed, as the years passed, was that I was getting old.

Came as sort of a surprise, don't you know. Here I thought I was immortal, and I wasn't.

The good news is that the martial arts can enable one to learn what immortality is, and thus achieve it.

First, I noticed that injuries made me rethink techniques. I would be unable to do some move because of an injury, and so I would adapt, and figure out a better way of doing that move.

A better way of moving the body.

Second, I realized that I was slowing down, and that I had to find a new way of thinking to keep any semblance of speed.

And, you can add power to this problem: I realized I didn't have the power I once had. The body was just…getting old.

Mind you, I was young, my mind seemed to be getting faster! But the body was old.

Time to jack it up.

But how do you jack up a body? Make it capable of keeping, and even increasing, youthful speed and power?

Technique.

And, behind the proper construction of technique, the proper construction of mind.

Third, I had to empty the mind of distractions. I had to 'go away' from thinking, and learn how to observe without the mind in the way.

What is the mind but a bunch of memories?

The good news is that realized that I had been doing everything right all along, I just had to focus enough so that I, the spirit, observed reality without the distractions of the mind in the way.

Do without emotion.

Do without attachments.

That sort of thing.

Fourth, I observed that, historically, the martial arts changed.

A couple of thousand years ago people were learning how to throw spears, fight with swords. There was not art.

They were cavemen, and then they began to learn, to practice with the tools they needed to survive.

They went through rough times, used clubs and threw rocks.

Then they found favorite clubs, shaped the clubs to fit their hands, to have better 'swingability.'

Then along came metal.

Do you understand? The martial arts didn't just pop into existence! They were formed by people over ages.

Take a look at China.

Hundreds of very polished fighting disciplines and, eventually, Tai Chi Chuan. The Grand Ultimate.

The grand ultimate in evolution, if you ask me.

Look at Japan.

Not as many fighting arts, very polished, but no Tai Chi.

Look at America.

A bunch of dopes who take polished fighting arts and reduce them to tournament techniques and trophies just to make a buck.

Sheesh.

Real cavemen, you know?

Yet, we are young, and the evolution is happening.

Now, let's shift the viewpoint a bit.

crude motion without thought
motion with a little thought
no motion…lots of thought

That is a rough representation of motion in the development of the martial arts. Historically speaking.

Go ahead, look at the various arts of the world, see if there is not somewhat of a mirror for this in every country, for all the arts.

It is rough, it is somewhat different in shape for each country, but there is a truth here.

Young men have motion, old men have thought.

Young arts have motion, old arts-and in this I mean polished arts-have less motion, or, if you wish, less effort.

Technique instead of anger.

So whether it is the person getting old, or merely the historical evolution of art through culture, you can see why, in the end, I felt I had to adapt Karate to Tai Chi Chuan.

I didn't need motion; I needed technique.

Now, there will be, doubtless, things that can be adjusted.

But if you adjust too far, you make Tai Chi, which has already been made.

If you don't adjust enough, you still have karate.

So we need to find a middle point, or at least a point that can be accepted as a useful 'next step' for the evolution of karate, without losing that which is uniquely karate.

An evolution that should aid in the understanding of all martial arts.

And now you understand why I obsess on shifting the body, rather than throwing it around.

Why I use fingertips, rather than bashing.

Still, some of the forms need no changing, just need to be appreciated as a more subtle tool for learning.

Usually, that will be in the techniques.

But, in the end, if you disagree with me and consider that I have done something wrong, if you just go back to the old throwing and bashing of classical karate, be it dumbed down or not, the simple fact will still remain.

You will get old.

You will get polished.

You will use more intelligence than power.

I just hope to get you there faster.

No bad me.

CHIANG NAN FOUR

Stand naturally, able to move in any direction without 'pre-leaning.'

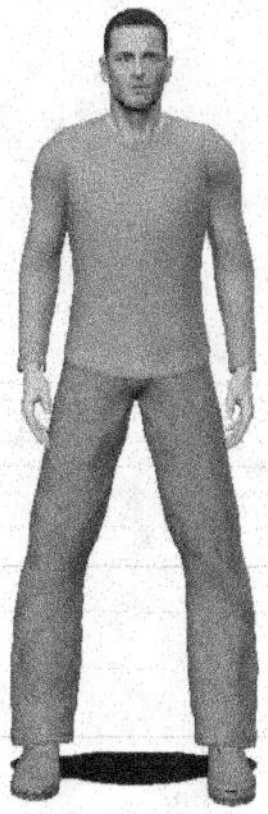

Pivot to the left 90 degrees as you cross the hands and bring them upwards.

Sink into a back stance.

The left hand executes an outward mid level position.

The right hand goes to the high position.

Pivot to the right 180 degrees as you cross the hands and bring them upwards.

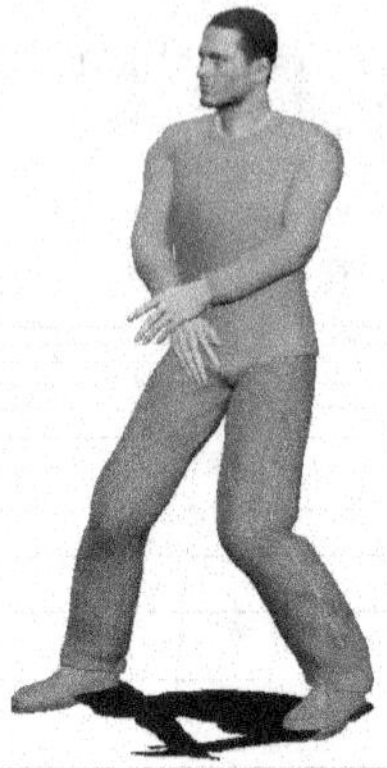

Sink into a back stance. The right hand executes an outward middle position. The left hand rises to the high position.

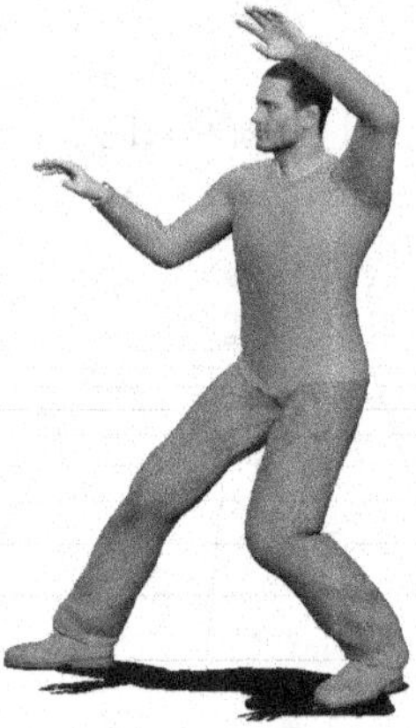

Bring the left foot up to the right and pivot 90 degrees into a cat stance. Rise the right hand slightly as you circle the left hand around to augment it.

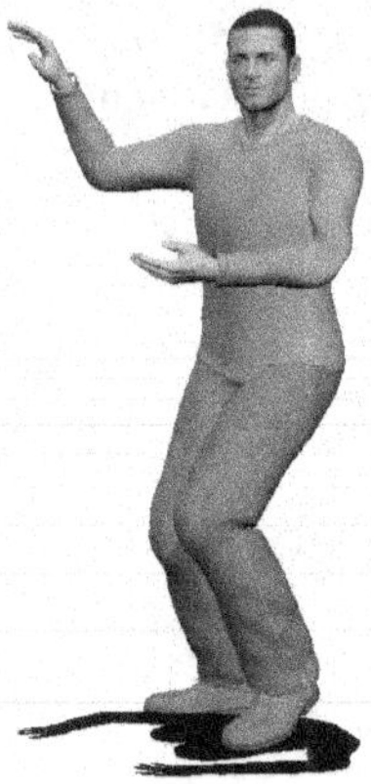

Step forward with the left foot into a front stance as you execute a crossed wrist low block.

Step back (switch step) with the left foot as you circle the right arm up and around, and the left hand down and around.

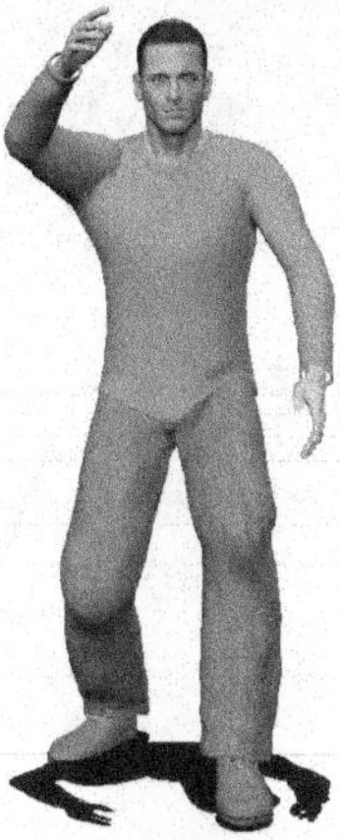

Step forward with the right foot into a cat stance, the left hand guarding the face and the right hand guarding the groin.

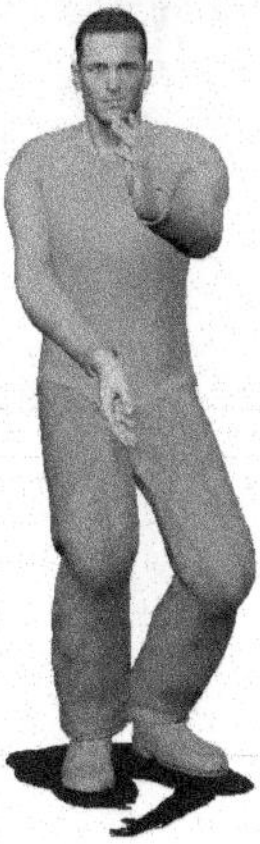

Step forward with the right foot into a front stance s you circle the right hand to an outward middle block. The left hand moves downward, in a smother block position.

Bring the left foot forward into a cat stance as you execute a left low block to the left and a right high block.

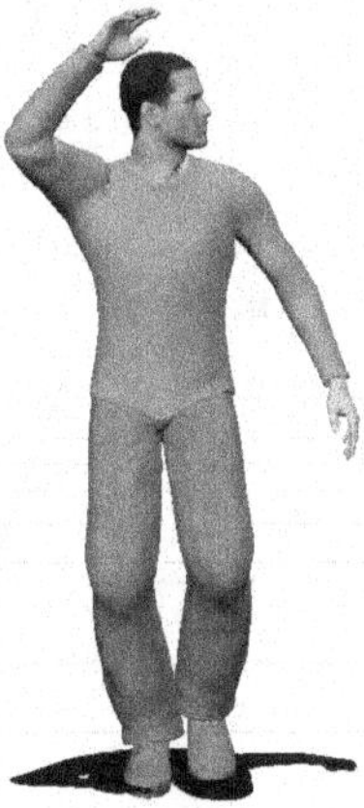

Pivot 90 degrees into a cat stance as you guard the face with the right hand and the groin with the left hand (parry).

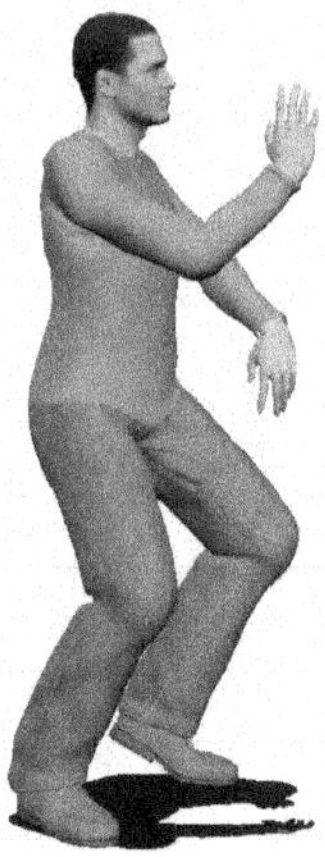

Execute a left front kick as you roll the right hand down to a parry and the left up to the middle outward block position.

This would be 'white snake' with a kick in Tai Chi.

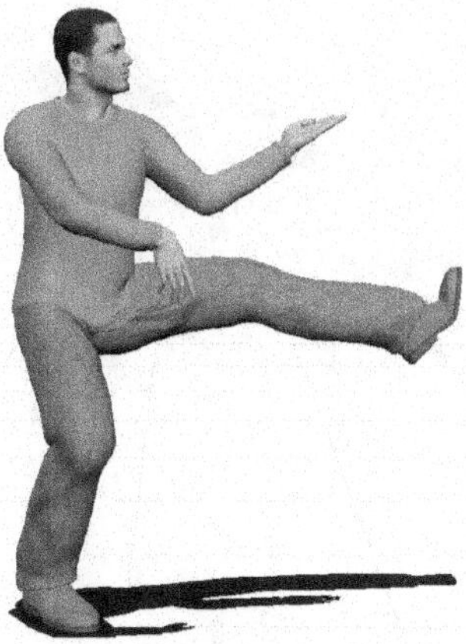

Set the left foot down in a front stance as you execute a right elbow to the left palm.

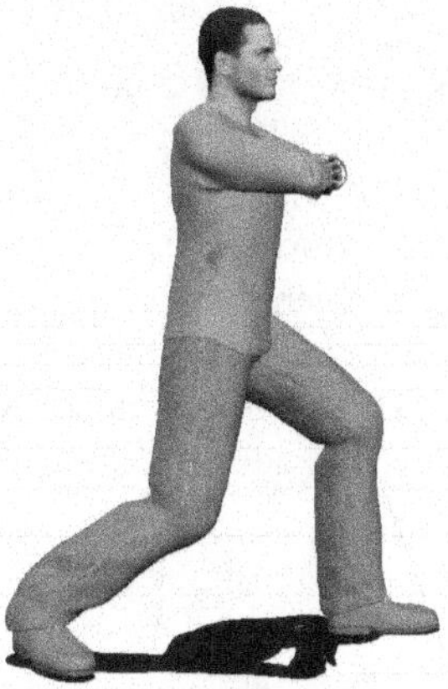

Bring the right foot next to the left foot and pivot 90 degrees to the right as you execute a right low block to the right and a left high block.

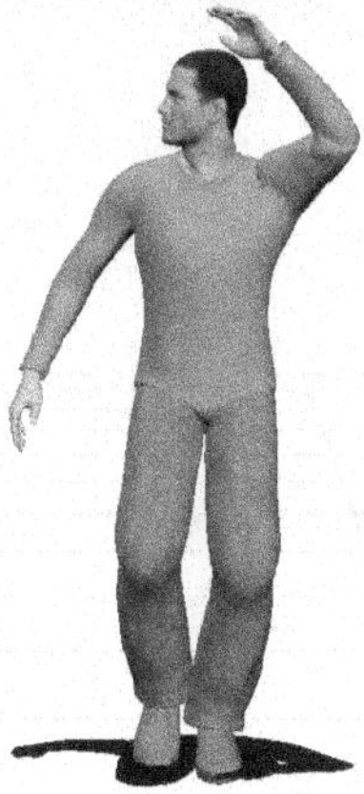

Pivot 90 degrees to the left into a cat stance as you guard the face with the left hand and the groin with the right (parry).

Execute a right front kick as you roll the left hand down and roll the right hand to the outward middle block position.

Remember, you are not do a 'side to side' block, you are shooting the block out from the tan tien to the side.

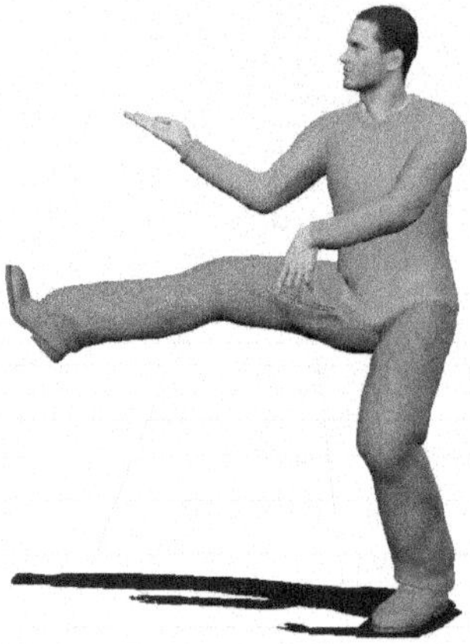

Set the right foot down in a front stance as you execute a left elbow to the right palm.

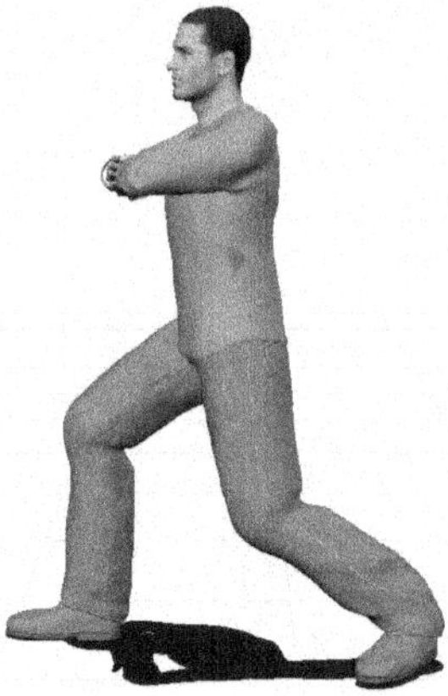

Bring the left foot up to the right and turn 90 degrees to the left into a reverse cat stance.

The left arm circles upward and the left arm circles downward.

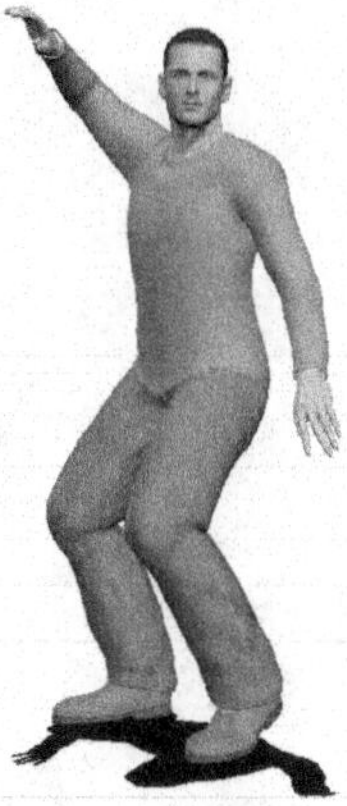

Turn the left foot out and step slightly forward and to the left with the right foot into a cat stance.

The right hand circles down to protect the groin. The left hand circles up to protect the face.

Execute a right front kick as the left hand circles down to a parry and the right hand circles up to a shooting middle block.

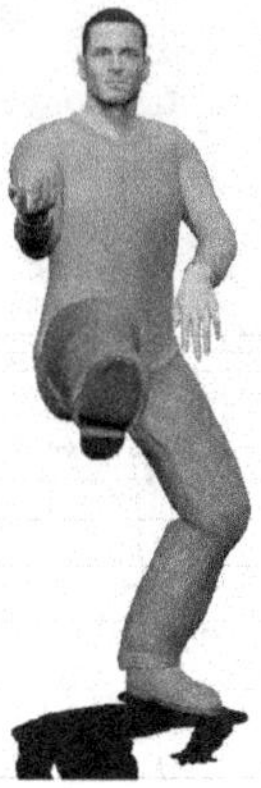

Set the foot down to the left, across the body, and begin pivoting 135 degrees to the left.

The arms should be scooping downward.

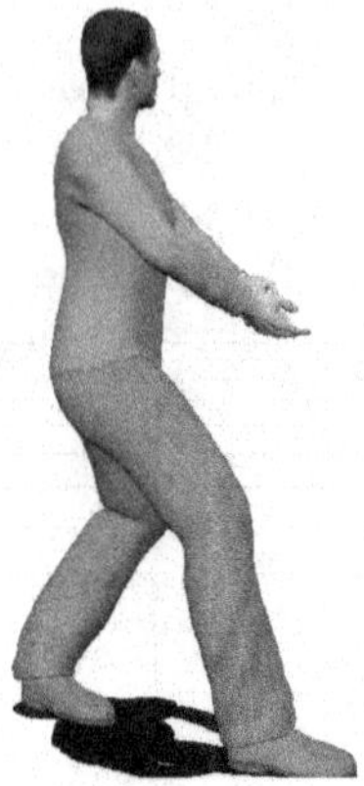

Pivot into a back stance. The arms should raise upward.

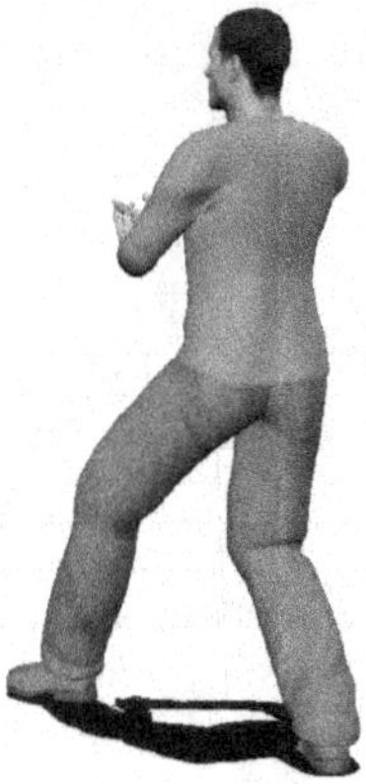

The arms turn over into the double outward grabbing position.

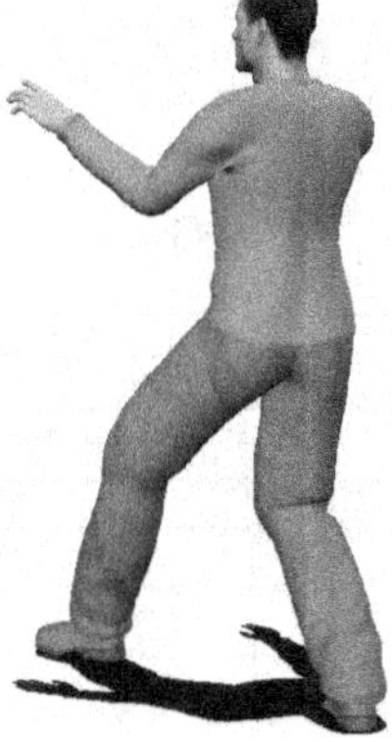

Execute a left front kick. The left palm guards the face.

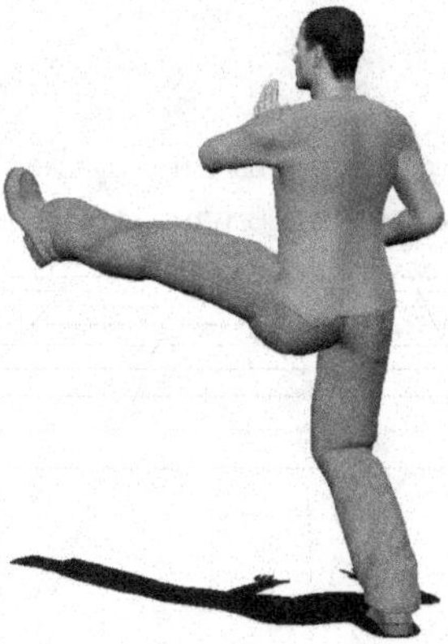

Set down in a front stance and execute a right reverse punch (spear hand).

Remember to square the hips.

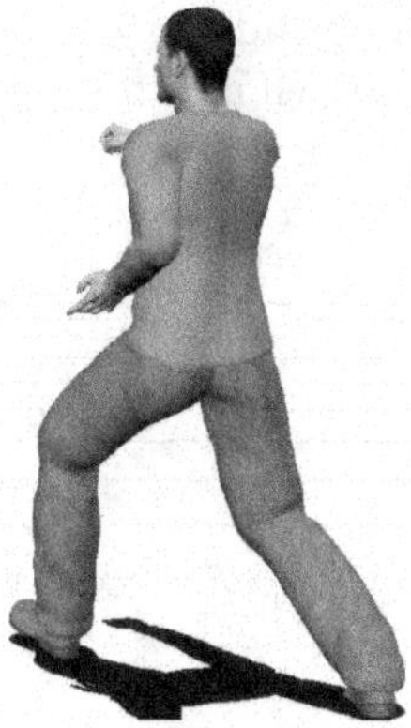

Execute a left punch (spear hand).

Remember to align the hips.

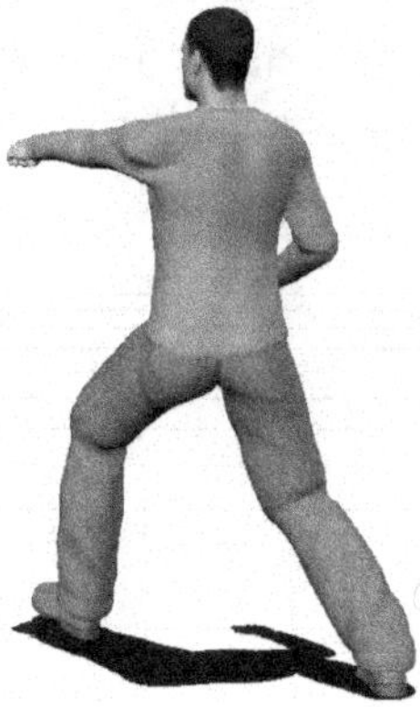

Step forward and turn to the right into a cat stance with the right foot as you scoop the hands in front of the body.

Bring the hands up, circle outward and down into the outward grabbing position.

Execute a right front kick. The right hand guards the face.

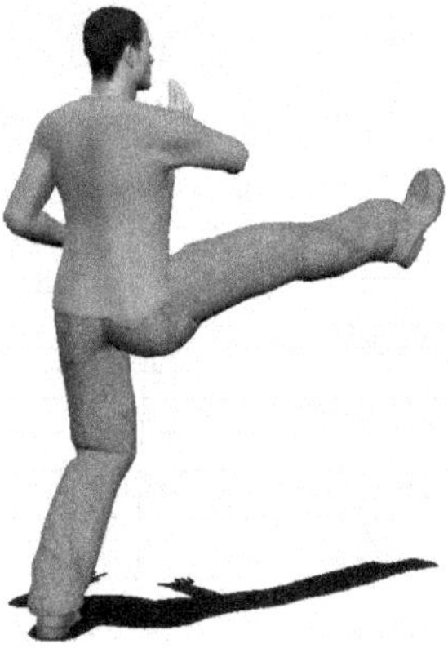

Set down in a front stance as you execute a left reverse punch (spear hand).

Execute a right punch (spear hand).

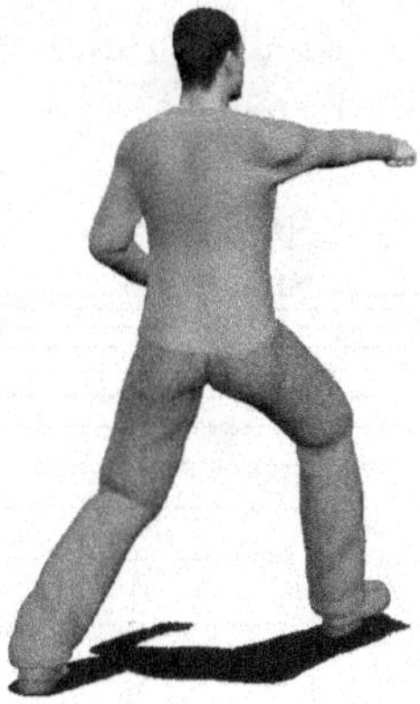

Step forward with the left foot and turn 45 degrees to the left into a cat stance.

The left hand guards the face and the right hand guards the groin.

Side view of last image.

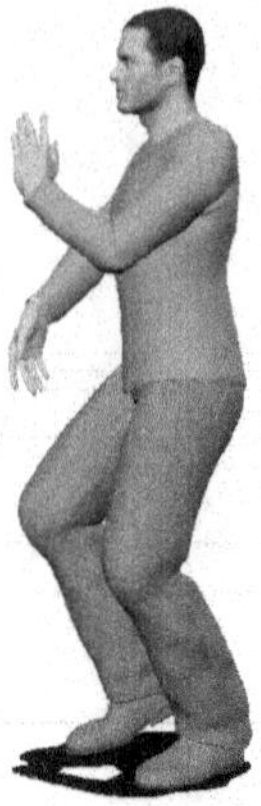

Move the left foot forward into a back stance as you roll the left hand down to a parry and the right hand up to the middle blocking position.

Side view of last image.

Step, shift into a front stance with the left foot as you shoot the hands forward.

The hands should be as if poking the eyes, but over the head as if grabbing the hair.

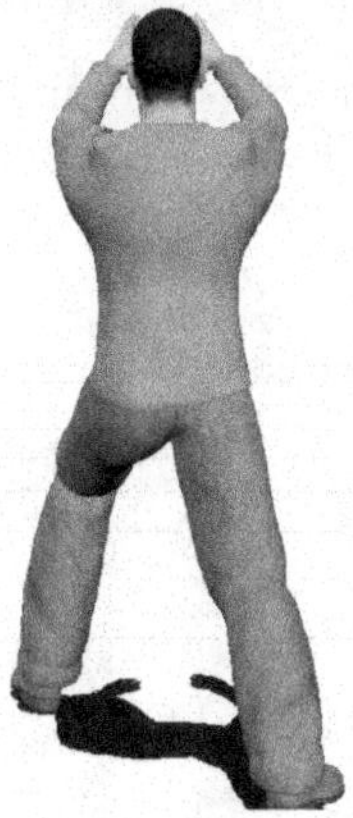

Side view of last image.

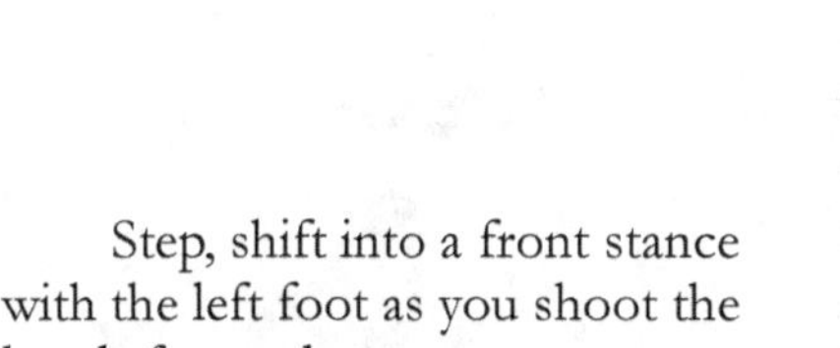

Bring the hands down and the right knee up, as if grabbing somebody's head and pulling it to knee them in the face.

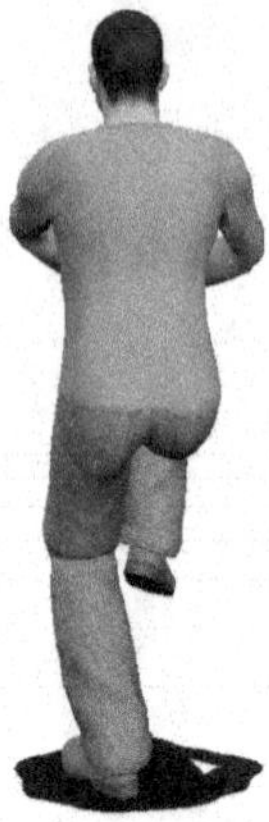

Side view of last image.

Set the left foot down to the right, across the body, and begin pivoting 180 degrees.

The hands should prepare for a double knife hand block.

Settle into a back stance with a left double knife hand block (outward grabbing).

Bring the right foot forward and assume the beginning position.

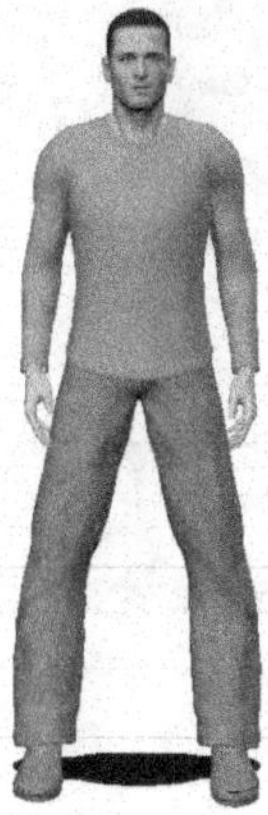

CHIANG NAN FOUR

APPLICATION FORTY-ONE

The attacker steps forward with the right foot and punches with the right hand.

The defender steps back with the right foot and guards the face with a left palm (slap).

The defender slaps the attacker's right hand into his left grab and pulls him as he moves forward, circling the left hand around the attacker.

Note the defender's position is exactly out of Chiang Nan four.

The defender keeps pulling the attacker forward and circles the left hand around the neck.

The defender hooks the attacker's chin with his left hand and starts pulling the attacker's head around to the left.

The defender pulls the attacker back, stretching the neck and hyper extending the attacker's arm.

NOTE

This is a technique requiring much subtlety, yet it it is, with a little practice, very easy to do.

It helps if the defender nudges the attacker's leg with his knee.

It resembles an Aikido throw, but is a bit more brutal in design.

There are many other options, should the technique degrade, simple chokes, sweeps, even arm locks.

APPLICATION FORTY-TWO

Kicks were not a large part of karate when it was invented. This was due to attire and armor, and probably other things.

Sweeps were practiced, but kicks were kept low, to the knees or the groin, at best.

Kicks came along in the middle of the last century. In particular, I remember Chuck Norris astounding the world by actually (choke) turning his back on an opponent to do a spin kick.

And to the head!

That said, kicks are in vogue now, and it would be silly of me not to address them in modern terms. Thus, here is a kick defense from Chiang Nan four.

This is from the third move, done after the second mid/high block, as the person is turning left to head up the center of the form. I don't lift the hand, as in the form, until after the technique is started.

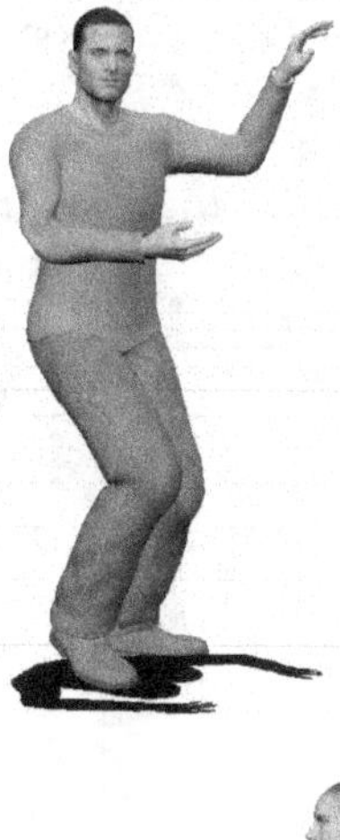

The attacker kicks with the right foot.

The defender steps back and hooks his left arm under the ankle.

The defender can lift the leg, step through and sweep with the right foot, even spin around with a back sweep with the right foot.

For this little tome, however, I am going to show you a technique I use, and with great effectiveness. It almost looks stupid, but I guarantee it works well with just a little practice.

How many of you have seen a foot caught, and the person who's foot is caught hops around the mat until he can get free?

So I don't do anything, I just lean a little closer, as if I couldn't turn the fellow on his head right then.

This invites a punch with the lead hand (the back hand is usually out of position and too awkward, anyway).

When the attacker punches I grab his right wrist with my right hand.

I then guide his punch down and place it in my left hand.

I now have the attacker in an 'arm/leg' twine, and I simply pull with my left hand, shove the foot with my left shoulder, and the fellow hits the mat hard, and in a way that, should I not show restraint, will crunch him bad.

And, if you don't like this technique, when you first grab his foot, smack the heel with your right palm and pop his body back in a way in which he won't be able to retain balance.

You can also move in and do a pubic punch (between the hip and the thigh) and the attacker will collapse.

APPLICATION FORTY-THREE

The attacker steps forward with the right foot as he punches with the right hand.

The defender smothers the strike down with a low crossed wrist block.

The defender grabs the attacker's right elbow with his right hand and pulls up.

The defender pushes down on the attacker's wrist with his left hand.

As the attacker bends to the pressure the defender snakes his left arm over the attacker's right arm. The attacker's right hand is in a good position for a wrist lock.

APPLICATION FORTY-FOUR

The attacker kicks with the right foot.

The defender steps forward into a front stance with the left foot and executes a crossed wrist low block.

The defender steps forward with the right foot into a front stance and executes a right upper cut to the chin.

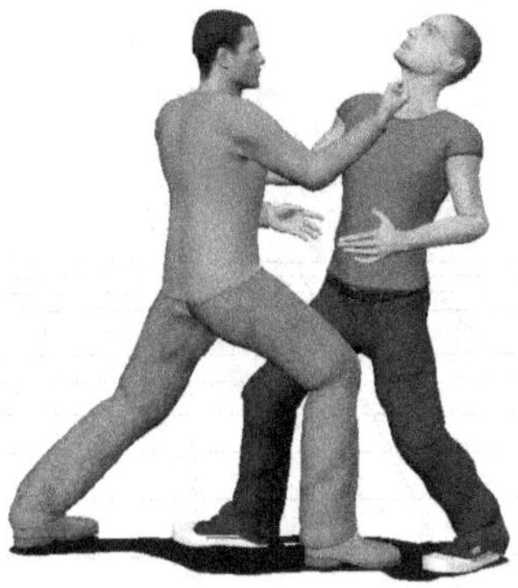

The essence of this technique is the speed to charge the body forward between the kick and the punch. This takes practice, but a good karate should have the body speed necessary to do this technique.

NOTE

Karate often touts the 'one strike one kill' philosophy. This is fine, but one should never stop with one strike; one should always utilize as many weapons as one has to the conclusion of the attacker laying on the ground, mangled, unconscious, etc. We don't advocate this expanded philosophy to the playground, but training should always be realistic and with the goal of the other fellow laying on the ground.

After the upper cut in this technique search for secondary attacks.

Can you end with a right sweep of the attacker's front foot?

How about just pushing his right knee with your right knee?

APPLICATION FORTY-FIVE

You'll find an old photo of Okinawans doing this technique, but they never show where it goes…the true technique.

The attacker steps forward with the right foot and punches with the right hand.

The defender executes a left parry.

The defender then executes a right back fist to the face, and a right kick to the groin.

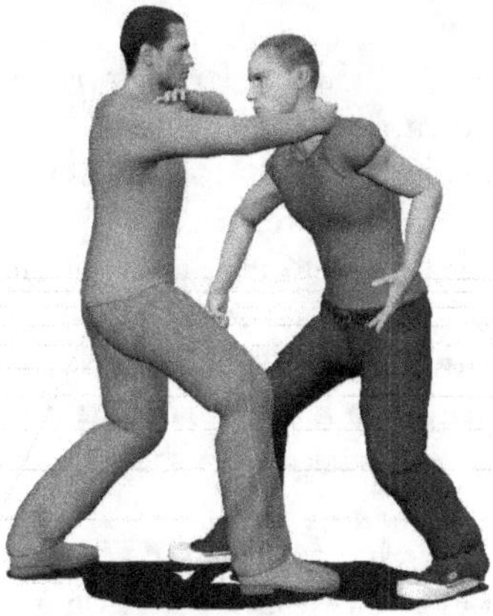

The defender sets forward in a front stance, grabs the attacker's neck with the right hand and pulls the attacker's head into a left horizontal elbow strike.

The defender circles the left arm to lift the attacker's arm. At the same time he pushes the head down, as if into the armpit.

You may have to shift the feet to make this technique work.

Done correctly, and with restraint, the attacker will end up sitting crosslegged in front go you.

Remember the value of 'shock and lock,' of striking an opponent so as to daze him and make him easier to manipulate.

APPLICATION FORTY-SIX

The attacker steps forward with the right foot and punches with the right hand.

The defender executes a right front kick and a right inward block.

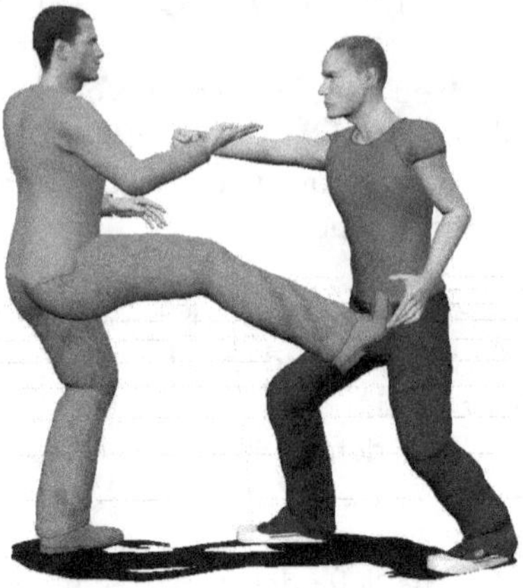

The defender stomps his foot down, brings his left foot up behind his right foot in a cross stance. The rear heel is up and the toes are pointing at the middle of the front foot. As the defender stomps he pulls the attacker's right arm with his left arm and executes a right back fist to the face.

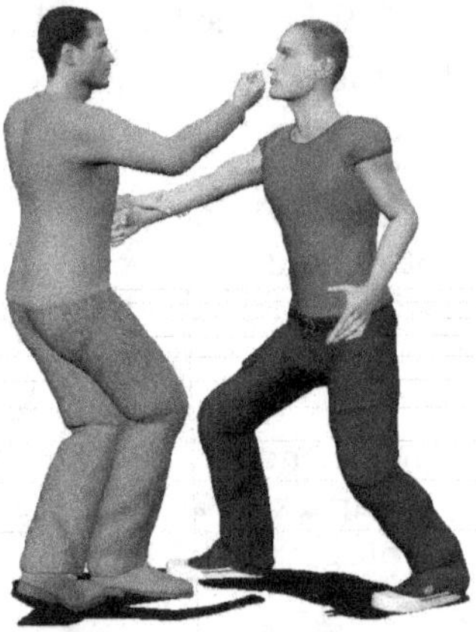

One can do the vertical arm pin at this point. I am going to diverge, however, so that I can discuss supercharging and chi power.

The defender raise his right knee.

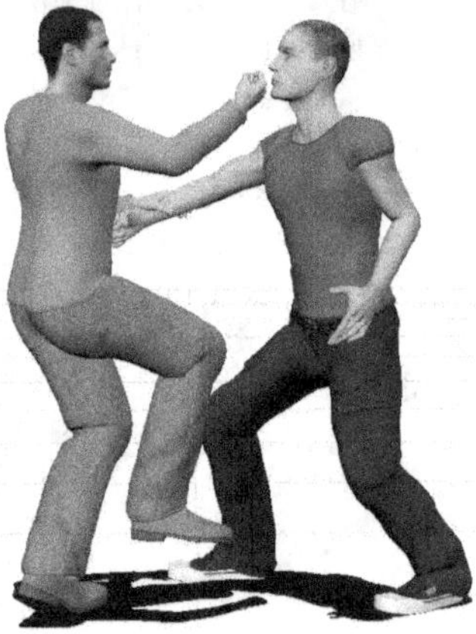

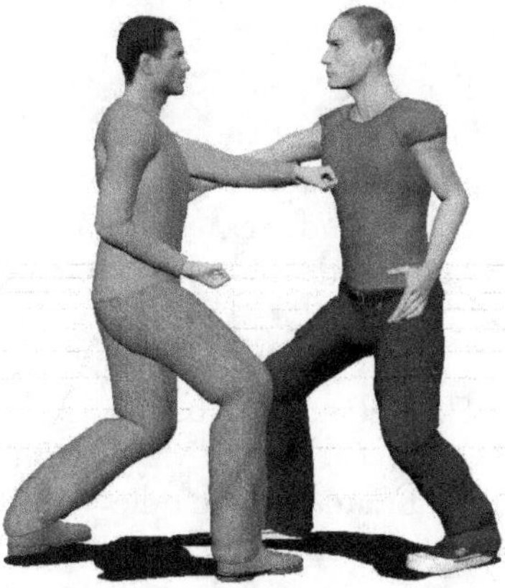

The defender stomps his right foot, assuming a front stance. His left foot shoots backward and to the left.

This is a 'supercharging' technique, and the defender strikes the attacker at the exact moment his foot contacts the ground.

NOTE

You can manufacture chi power by treating your body like a machine.

The lower the stance, the harder you work, the more the tan tien glows, the more chi power you have.

When you supercharge you stomp the foot hard, but not hard enough to harm the foot. When the foot contacts the ground the weight of the body is increased and the tan tien will work even harder. The energy it creates can be channeled through the body into the technique.

To understand supercharging, and chi power, for that matter, one must dedicate himself to the basic-basics: breathing, relaxing, grounding, body alignment, Coordinated Body Motion (CBM).

Further, one should study the three powers: thrusting the weight of the body, rotating the hips, grounding the weight.

When one moves every part of the body at the same time, including the proper proportions of thrusting, rotating and gravity, then chi power emits.

The odd thing is that you have to be relaxed when you do this, which seems to be contrary, but isn't. In the body energy simply flows better through that which is empty than that which is full.

APPLICATION FORTY-SEVEN

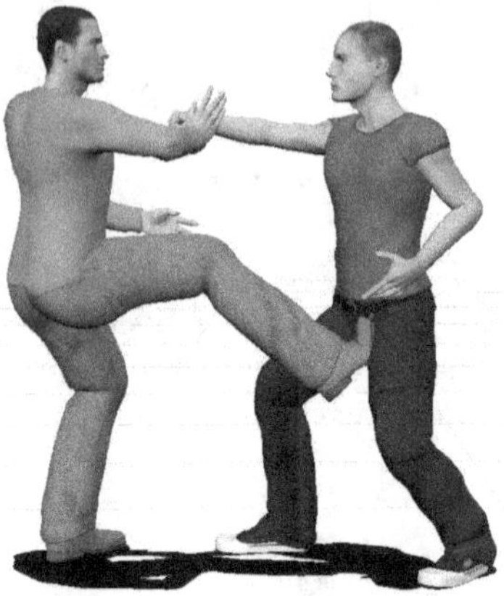

The attacker steps forward with the right foot and punches with the right hand.

The defender executes a right palm block and a right kick to the groin.

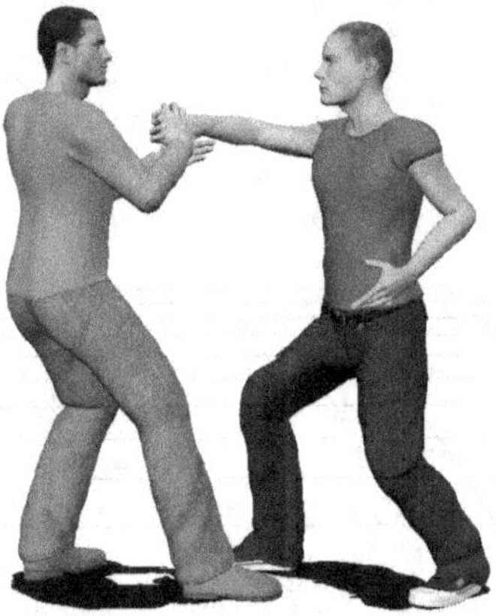

The defender grabs the attacker's fist. The best way is with the thumb under the middle knuckle, but there are several ways to grip the hand. While the technique can be done with one hand, beginners should use two hands.

The defender turns the wrist over.

The technique can be done in either direction, turning the wrist one way, or the other.

You can turn the attacker into an arm bar, or with the elbow bent, but you should be able to control the attacker. You should be able to move him up, down, either side; you should be able to move his body, using only the wrist, in any direction you please.

APPLICATION FORTY-EIGHT

The attacker steps forward with the right foot and punches with the right hand.

The defender assumes a back stance and stops the punch with a left palm/stop to the biceps.

The attacker throws a left punch to the face.

The defender steps/shifts forward into a front stance and shoots both hands towards the face.

This could be fingers to the eyes, but in the interest of not crippling stupid people we will just shoot past the face and grab the back of the head, shoulders, ears, hair, whatever.

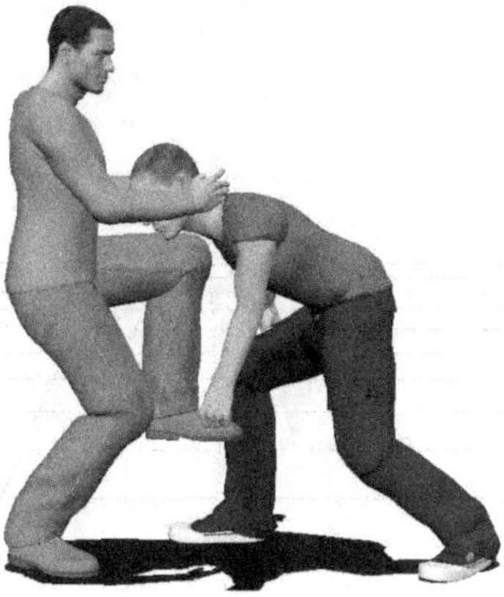

The defender shifts back and pulls the attacker's head down with his entire weight. He executes a left knee strike to the face.

If the attacker manages to block the attack, or is still standing, the defender can always use elbows, to the back of the neck.

CONCLUSION TO THE PROMISE FIGHTS OF CHIANG NAN FOUR

To master the martial arts you must practice until you don't have to think about what you are doing.

First, you can do this with the forms. Practice them until you just do them, never have to think about the next move.

Second, practice the applications until they are intuitive, no thought necessary.

Third, practice freestyle (especially drills) until you don't have to think about what you are doing. You must focus on your opponent, and refuse ANY distractions.

What you are trying to do is get rid of the mind.

The mind is memory.

People say certain things are the result of your mind, your mental abilities.

This is not true.

The mind is just a storehouse of memories, and the real action in this subject is you, the spirit, the 'I am.'

Your mind does nothing (except, perhaps, throw up distractions), it is you who do everything.

Sixth sense, paranormal, seeing what is going to happen before it happens, telekinesis…everything that is not explainable by science…is the result of you.

You are beyond the short-sighted science of mankind.

The science of mankind only measures occurrences of the universe.

Science can never explain what a spirit is.

Science can never explain you.

This is what the martial arts are about: learning to focus so well that your mind, or other distractions, do not intrude upon your ability to concentrate.

Chapter Seven
Chiang Nan Five

Below are the videos for form Five.

channan 5 explained ~ https://youtu.be/15Rfh6CTFNQ	4:18
channan 5 ~ https://youtu.be/YiJa9x2Lup8	2:10
channan 5 side ~ https://youtu.be/XqDwY1tDa9U	1:38
channan 5 app 22 ~ https://youtu.be/oD8PvQxQ0rQ	3:26
channan 5 app 23 ~ https://youtu.be/vIU5DysJrmY	6:35
channan 5 app 24 ~ https://youtu.be/wxEbtU6O5D0	3:49
channan 5 app 25 ~ https://youtu.be/Fl-nynFB7dY	4:36
channan 5 app 26 ~ https://youtu.be/JFIopNM-H0A	7:39
channan 5 app 27 ~ https://youtu.be/xHI_rvt3_bk	10:00
channan 5 app 28 ~ https://youtu.be/eRhEQeb7rAE	2:06
channan 5 app 29 ~ https://youtu.be/9tptIUgSc5I	5:00
channan 5 app 30 ~ https://youtu.be/L74_uwR2Yio	3:57
channan 5 app 31 ~ https://youtu.be/So2igBpvASk	7:31
channan 5 app 32 ~ https://youtu.be/h6ojTVwY90E	2:56
	56:34

Chiang Nan Five

I came into this game of translating karate into tai chi with certain advantages.

I had a base in engineering, my father was an engineer and didn't truck with fanciful philosophy.

I had a talent for writing, my mother was an English teacher and didn't waste time with sloppy writing.

And I had one grandmother a Latin teacher, and one grandfather a judge. I had a built in respect for history and how it should actually be used to shape one's thought processes.

The martial arts, however, were different than any of the subjects listed above. Which was good, for it gave me a field in which to exercise all of those subjects.

I developed matrixing.

Matrixing is a scientific viewpoint. A logic.

It is used to put order in the martial arts, and to order the progression of study, among other things.

When I was studying Kenpo, back in 1967, I had the cognition that that body was two halves, right and left.

And that each half had two sides; each side could be opened or closed.

As the years went by I extrapolated upon this type of thought.

Up, down…side to side…I tried to organize the moves of the martial arts to the various potentials of motion.

One can move the body in different directions.

Up, down, right, left, forward, back.

So when I looked at techniques I would analyze that by trying each of the six motions, then seeing what the hands and feet needed to do.

That proved useful, but it left me with a bigger problem.

You can adapt the six directions to the various blocks.

I would step in one of the six ways, then look at which of the six ways I could move my hands (or feet).

If I had a middle block, should I move it up, down, left, right, forward, back?

This was quite useful, and it led to my understanding the various hand configurations. I now understood what body motion would go with a hook, a parry, a hard block, a finger jab, and so on.

Which, of course, led to other problems.

Chief among the problems was distance.

Kick, punch, knee, elbow. Grappling. Weapons.

These were the six items necessary to understanding if I was going to master the martial arts.

I found if I could control distance I could control a fight.

I found that students who were afraid of 'bumping the body' had a far more difficult time of learning a technique than those who weren't so afraid.

I began to see the differences between arts.

I began to see how arts were pure…before they were corrupt.

That is, an art would grow out of a concept. When it reached a certain stage, it would collide with other arts; the concepts of one art didn't always mesh with concepts of other arts.

So I began matrixing entire arts, searching for the original concepts, and in the refining came my polish. Consider the following points.

Polish is not a result of how much you know.

Polish is putting aside distractions and focusing on just the technique at hand.

Polish is, therefore, in an odd way, 'how little you know.'

If you can 'not know' distractions, if you can create your own intense little universe, if you can put aside the agreed reality of all and focus, instead, upon constructing your own reality, then you will have polish, and your reality will hold sway over the reality of others.

Now, just to let you know, I have written MUCH on matrixing, and what you have read here is just the barest of thumbnails.

Good skill to you.

CHIANG NAN FIVE

Stand in the natural stance.

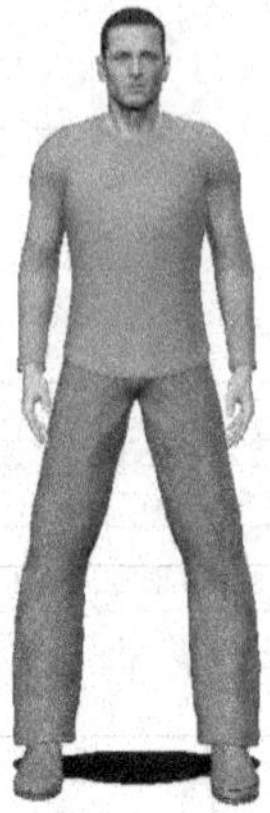

Pivot to the left into a back stance as you protect the face with a right palm block (slap).

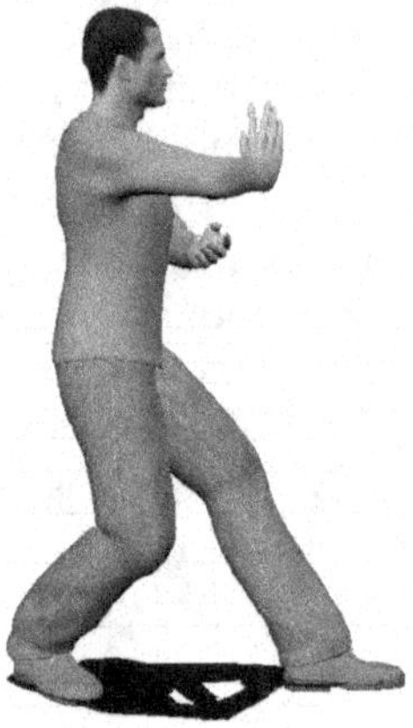

Pivot slightly to the right as you execute a left knife hand (grab).

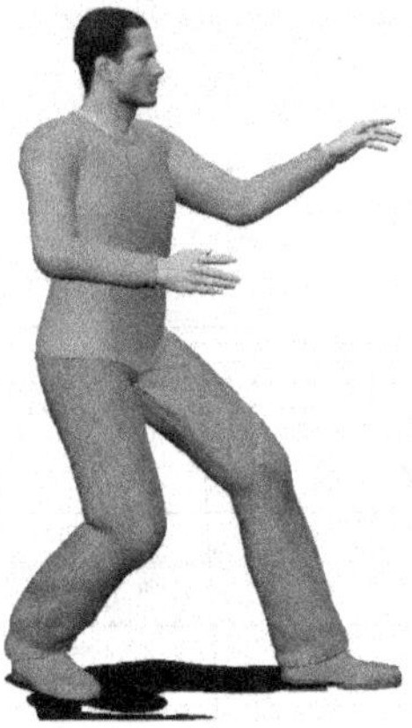

Execute a right spear hand.

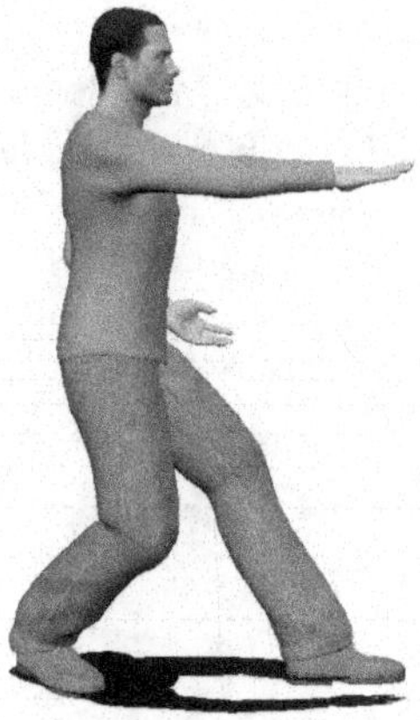

Bring the left foot back to the right as you pivot 90 degrees to the right. The right arm stays extended and the left arm crosses the body, palm up, to the elbow. The knees should be bent.

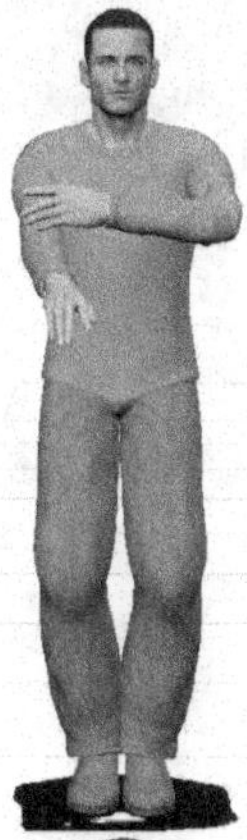

Straighten the knees as you retract the right hand, turn the left hand palm down, and look to the right.

Pivot to the right into a back stance as you execute a left palm block (slap).

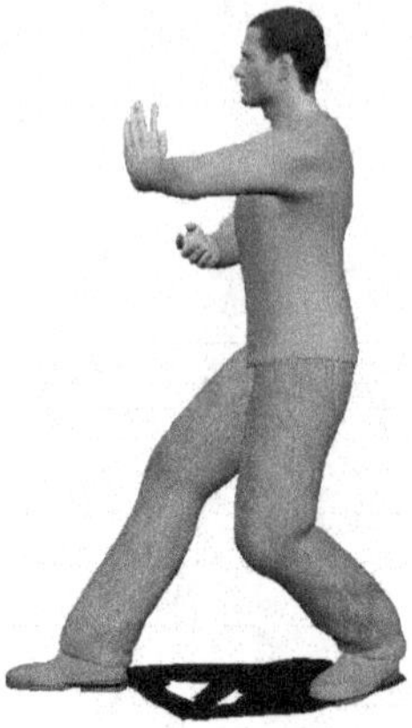

Pivot slightly to the left as you execute a right knife hand (grab).

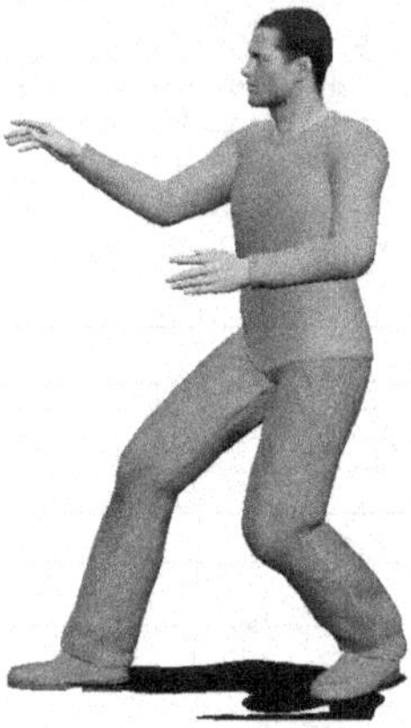

Execute a left spear hand.

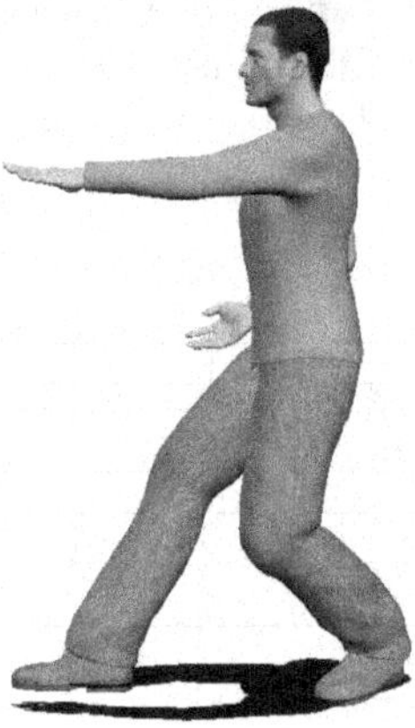

Bring the right foot back to the left as you pivot 990 degrees to the left. The left arm stays extended and the right arm crosses the body palm up to the elbow.

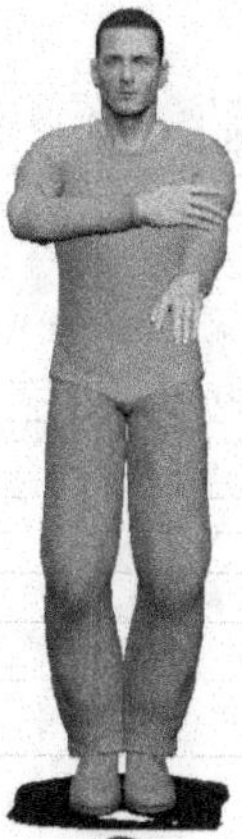

Straighten the legs as you retract the left arm and turn the right hand palm down.

Start to bend the knees as you move the right arm up and the left hand down.

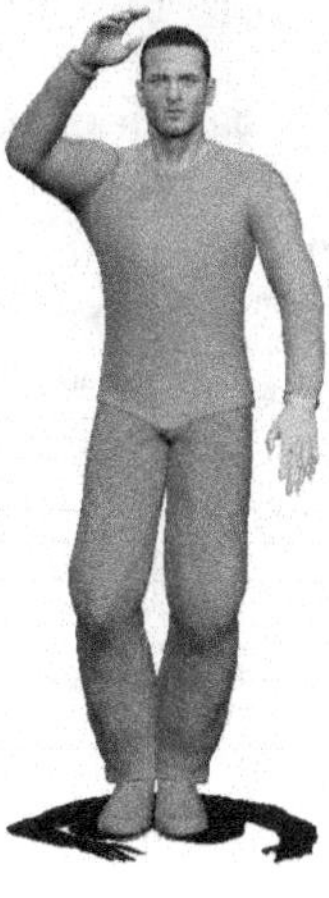

Continue to bend the knees as you continue the motion of the arms and circle them. The left palm guards the face and the right palm guards the groin.

Step forward with the right foot into a front stance as you execute a right outward block with the palm up.

Bring the right foot back and switch step to step forward with the left foot into a front stance with a low crossed wrist block. The hips should be square to the front.

Step/shift back into a back stance as you execute a high crossed wrist block.

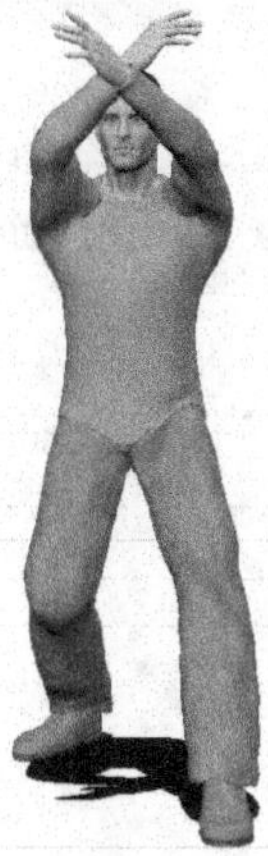

Lower the hands in a crossed smother block.

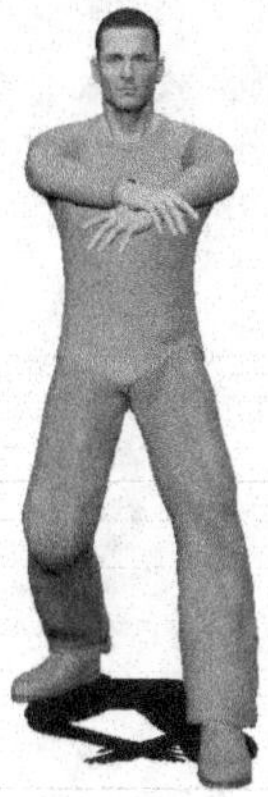

The right hand parries downward, the left hand rolls inside.

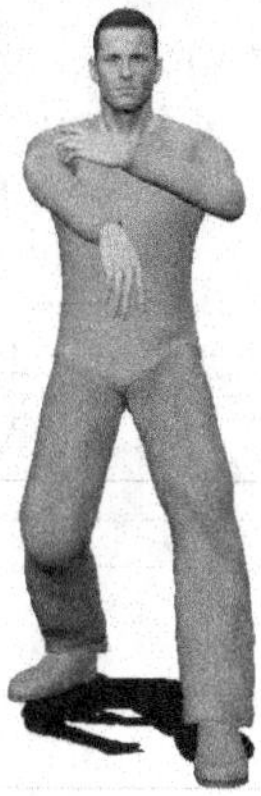

The right hand chambers, the left hand rolls to the middle position.

The left foot retracts to a cat stance as the left arm circles outward in a switch step.

The right foot steps forward into a front stance as you execute a right spear hand to the front.

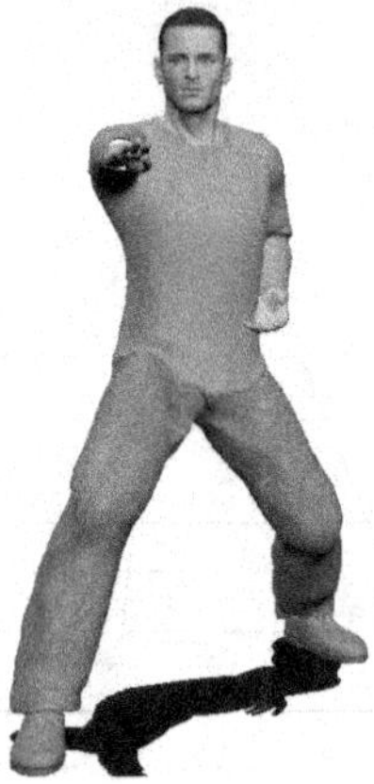

Step to the left with the right foot, in front of the left foot, and pivot 180 degrees into a back stance. The right arm swings around in an extended palm block.

Side view of last image.

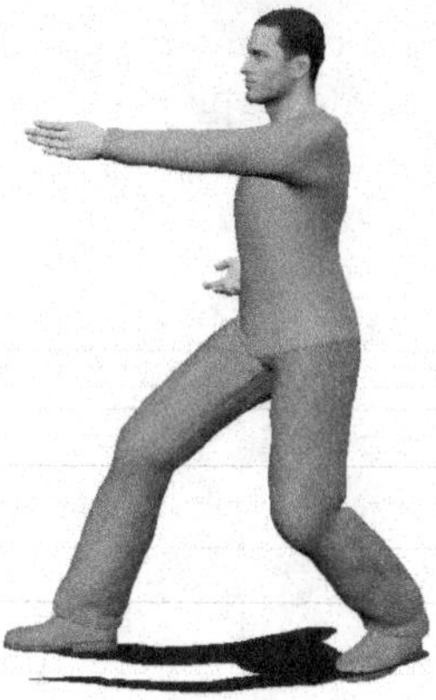

Retract the right hand and extend the left hand in a vertical spear.

Side view of last image.

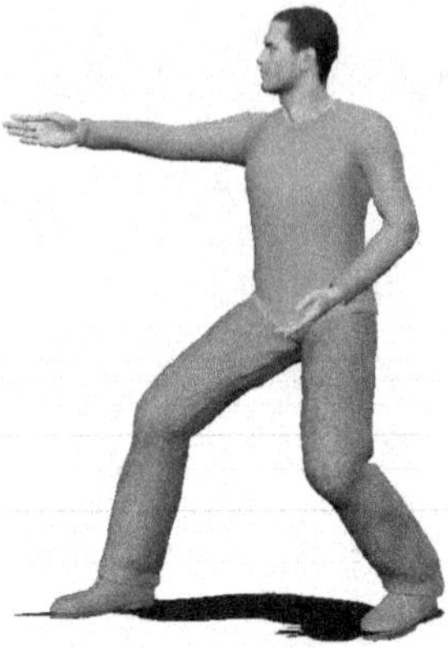

Swing the right knee and the right arm in a 'sweeping' block.

Side view of last image.

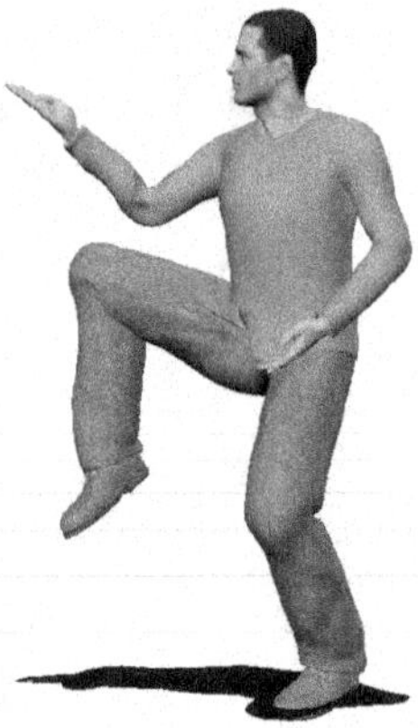

Set the right foot down in a horse stance with a right open hand low block.

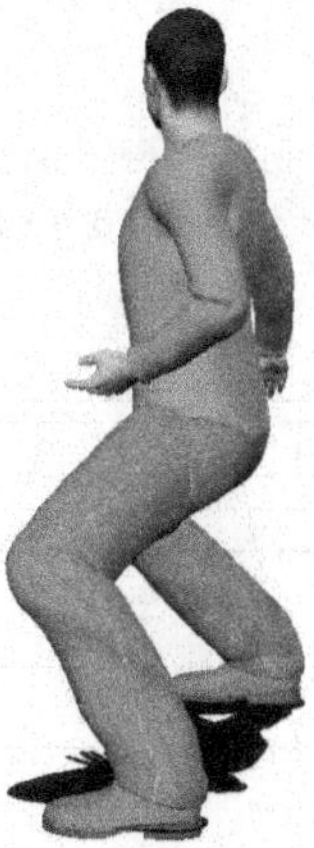

Side view of last image.

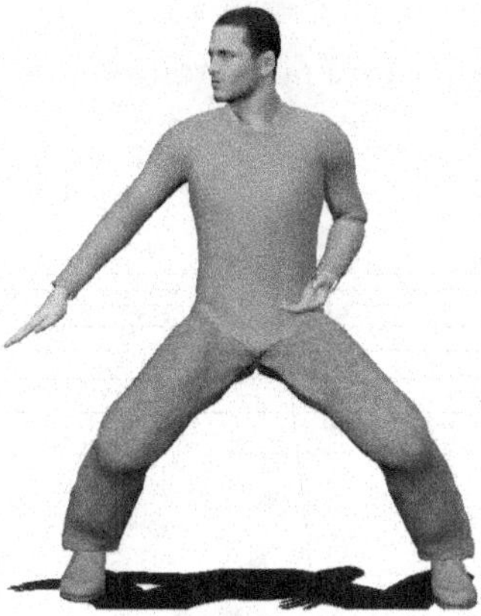

Pivot 180 degrees to the left in a back stance with an extended palm block.

Retract the right hand and extend the left hand in a vertical spear thrust.

Execute a right crescent kick to the left palm.

Set the right foot down in a horse stance as you strike the left palm with a right horizontal elbow.

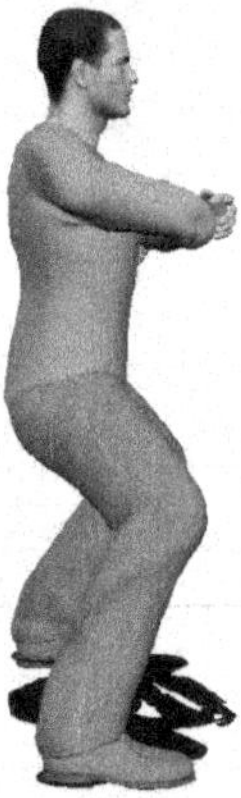

Bring the right foot next to the left foot as you raise the right arm and lower the left arm.

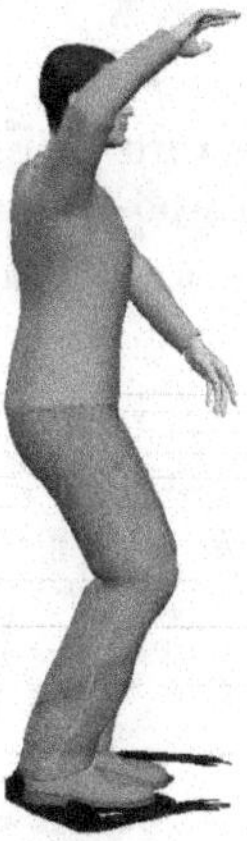

Continue the circle of the hands as you pivot 90 degrees to the right into an X stance. The left palm should guard the face, the right palm should guard the groin.

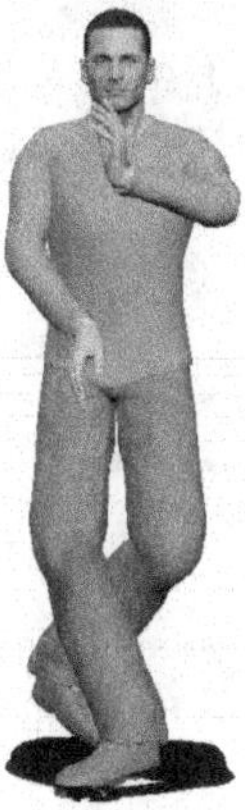

Raise the right knee as you execute a right outward block with the palm up.

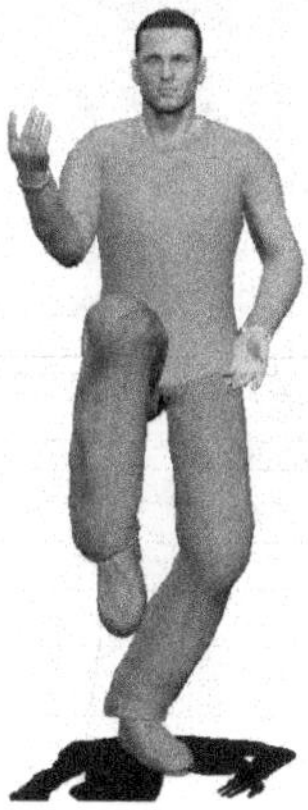

Step forward with the right foot into a front stance as you execute a left horizontal spear thrust.

Bring the left foot behind the right foot in an X stance.

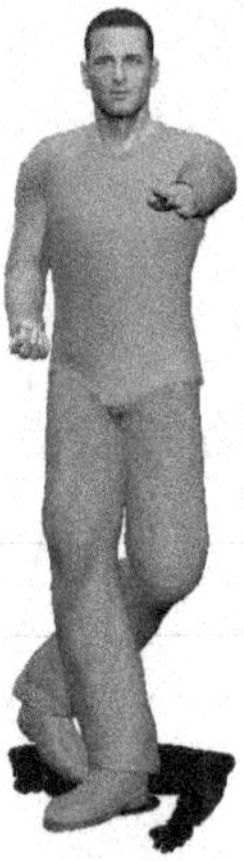

Pivot 180 degrees to the left into a X stance as you execute a low crossed wrist block.

Side view of last image.

Begin stepping forward with the right foot as you begin circling the right arm up and the left arm down.

Side view of last image.

Continue stepping with the right foot to a cat stance. The arms should circle until the left palm guards the face and the right arm guards the groin.

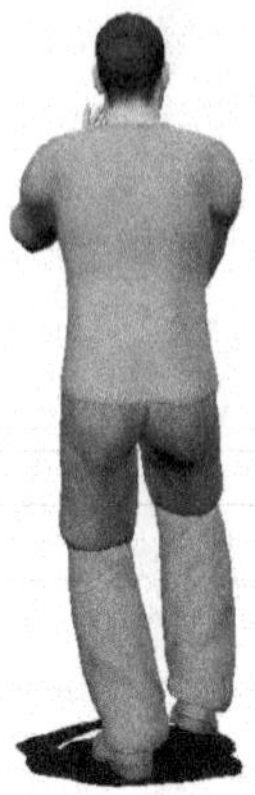

Side view of last image.

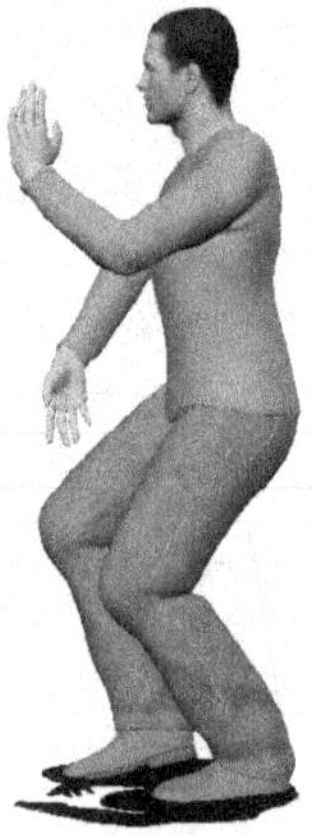

Step forward with the right foot into a front stance as you execute a right outward grabbing block.

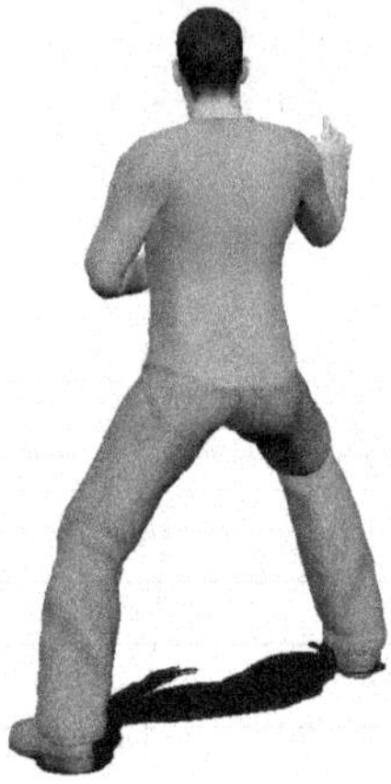

Bring the left foot up to the right as you pivot 90 degrees to the left. The right hand executes an upward block and the left hand executes a low block to the side.

Pivot 180 degrees to the left in an X stance as you execute a left high block and a right low block.

Step forward with the right foot into a front stance as you execute a right palm block and a left palm up spear thrust (as if to the groin).

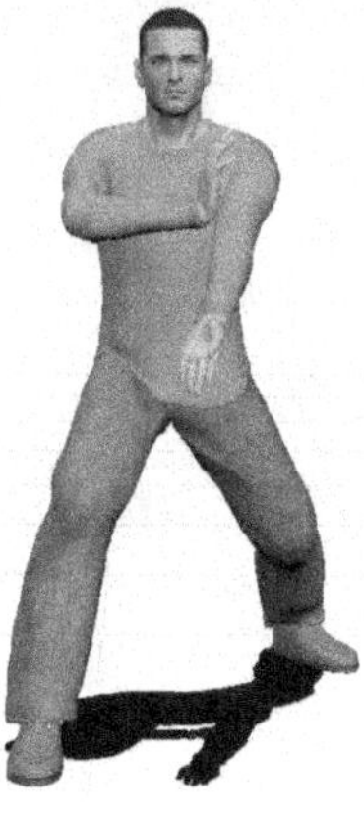

Bring the right foot back next to the left as you pivot 90 degrees to the left. The left arm executes a high block and the right arm executes a low block.

Return to the natural stance.

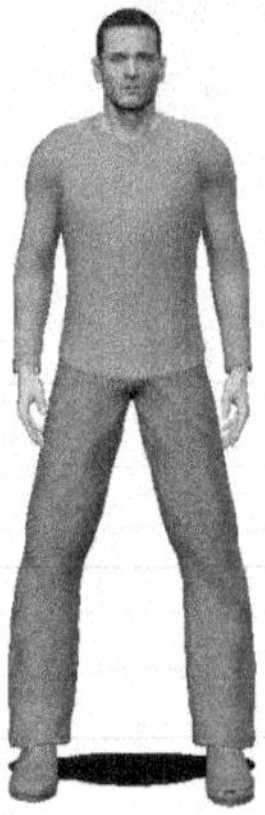

CHIANG NAN FIVE

APPLICATION FORTY-NINE

The attacker steps forward with the left foot and punches with the left hand.

The defender steps back with the right foot into a back stance and executes a right palm block.

The palm is a slap.

The attacker punches with the right hand.

The defender pivots slightly to the right as he executes a left knife hand block (grab).

The defender pulls the attacker's right hand as he executes a right spear hand to the throat or eyes.

APPLICATION FIFTY

The attacker steps forward with the left foot and punches with the left hand.

The defender steps back with the right foot into a back stance as he executes a right palm (slap).

The defender steps/shifts/shuffles forward into a front stance as he executes a left mid-level block with the palm up.

The attacker is thrown over the defender's left leg.

This is a splitting technique.

Other options appear: grabbing the leg to help the toss, punching the kidney, sweeping the lead leg with the left leg, and so on.

NOTE

This technique is common to tai chi chuan. A simple ward off, then slant flying.

Did the Okinawans have it? Doubtless in some form, but it is one of those neglected moves, stumbled upon but rarely passed down in Karate.

The problem is that Karate tends to favor the fist, so why push somebody over the leg when you can punch them so hard their armor cracks?

APPLICATION FIFTY-ONE

The attacker steps forward with the left foot and punches with the left hand.

The defender steps back with the right foot into a back stance as he executes a left cross palm block (slap).

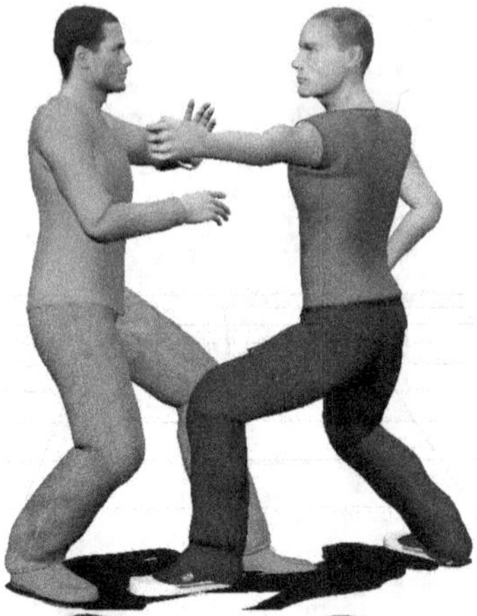

The defender circles outward with the right hand to do an outward grabbing block.

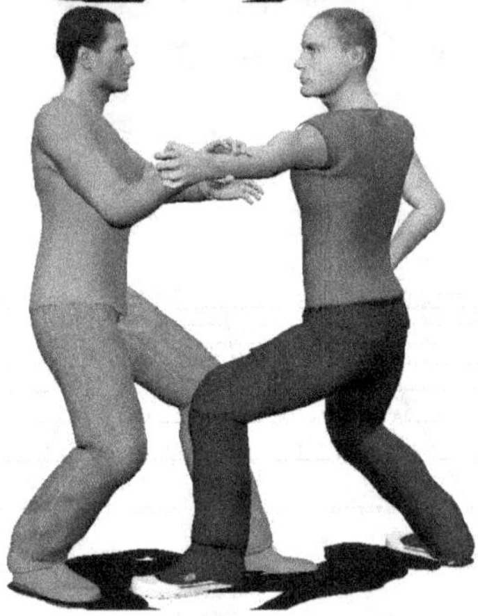

The defender steps/shift/shuffles forward into a front stance. He pulls the attacker's left arm down and inserts the left arm under the arm and executes an outer block with the palm up.

This technique is common to Aikido, but is in many other arts. It is a splitting technique. It is also what you do when you wish to use 'slant flying' on the off side.

APPLICATION FIFTY-TWO

The attacker kicks with the right foot.

The defender steps forward with the left foot, jamming the foot, and blocking with a crossed wrist low block.

The defender grabs the heel with his right hand, and pushes down on the foot with the left hand.

As the foot turns the defender snakes his left arm under and over and wraps the ankle. This is like a wrist twist, but with the ankle, I call it 'foot catcher.'

There are MANY options for catching and turning kicks.

In the end, you will realize that though it is important to have good kicks, kicks are easy to defend against.

If you block with the wrong leg forward, or the wrong arm on top, you will have to shift back to protect the head and execute a left inward middle block.

APPLICATION FIFTY-THREE

The attacker steps forward with the right foot and chops straight down towards the crown of the defender's head.

The defender rushes forward with the left foot into a front stance and catches the attacker's right wrist.

The defender pulls the wrist down with his right hand, and rolls the left wrist so as to apply pressure to the attacker's elbow with his left forearm.

This is a classic with many variations.

It is especially useful for teaching beginning knife or sword disarms.

If you step forward with the wrong foot, or have the wrong hand on top, you are open to a left punch. In this case you should shift into a back stance and execute a right downward outward block (the biceps are an especially good target), and then power up an armor crunching left punch to the chest.)

APPLICATION FIFTY-FOUR

The attacker steps forward with the right foot and chops downward with the right hand.

The defender rushes forward into a front stance with the left foot. He executes a high crossed wrist block.

The defender sweeps the attacker's hand down and to the left (opening the attacker) with his right hand. The left hand prepares for the next move.

The defender pivots into a horse stance as he executes a left chop to the throat.

The defender steps/pivots into a front stance as he executes a right punch to the chest.

NOTE

This was the original Kang Duk Won technique. I changed it (to the previous technique, number 53, in this book) for various strategic reasons.

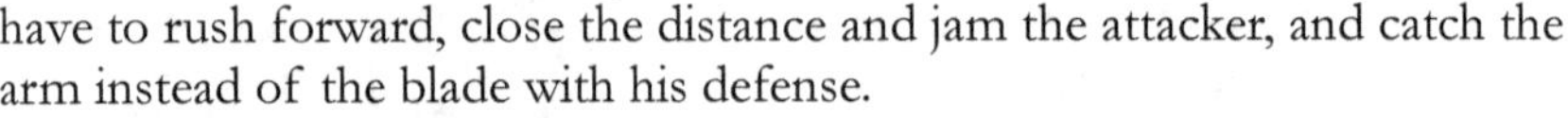

One thing of note is that in a technique that simulates weapons, or even feet, the defender might have to rush forward, close the distance and jam the attacker, and catch the arm instead of the blade with his defense.

One thing I do that is sometimes hard to see is push forward with my front knee against the knee of the attacker. This unbalances the attacker and is VERY useful for destroying an attack.

APPLICATION FIFTY-FIVE

The attacker executes a left front kick (could be a side or wheel or whatever).

The defender raises the left knee and the left arm to check the kick.

The attacker sets his foot down and the defender executes a left side kick.

Optional techniques would include stomping the knee.

I am not a fan of high kicks. I believe in training high, but I believe in kicking low, taking out the knees, the groin, whatever.

Still, this is a matter of personal preference, and in a real situation one would use whatever is appropriate.

APPLICATION FIFTY-SIX

The attacker steps forward with the left foot and punches with the right hand.

The defender executes a left crescent kick to the wrist.

The defender executes a side kick. A wheel kick is also an option.

It is useful to hop, and thus supercharge, a kick. This is especially true if somebody has managed to catch one of your feet. You can throw the weight and roll away, he shouldn't be able to hold your whole body weight, or just hop and pop the hips into the kick.

NOTE

I have always believed that the hands should be as powerful as the feet, and the feet should be as flexible as the hands. By this time in a student's training they should be realizing that. I recommend thousands of kicks per day to pursue this reality.

BTW, some people hold that the crescent kick is good for kicking the knife out of an attacker's hands. I had an instructor, normally brilliant, who tried that little brain fart. He managed to get a dozen stitches at the local hospital.

APPLICATION FIFTY-SEVEN

The attacker steps forward with the left foot and punches with the left hand.

The attacker steps forward with the left foot into a horse stance. He catches the attacker's left wrist with his right hand and executes a left elbow to the face.

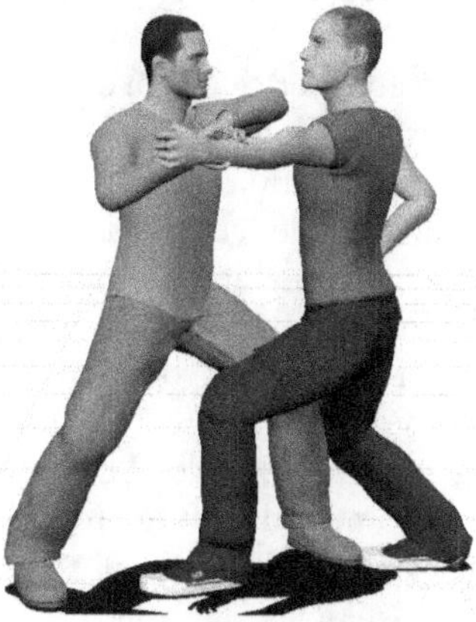

The defender extends his left arm next to the attacker's neck.

The defender steps forward with the right foot as he pushes down on the attacker's neck with his left hand and pushes the attacker's right arm diagonally up and around. This results in a vertical arm pin.

By this point in their training the student should be able to step into an attack and merely grab the attack without recourse to the slap.

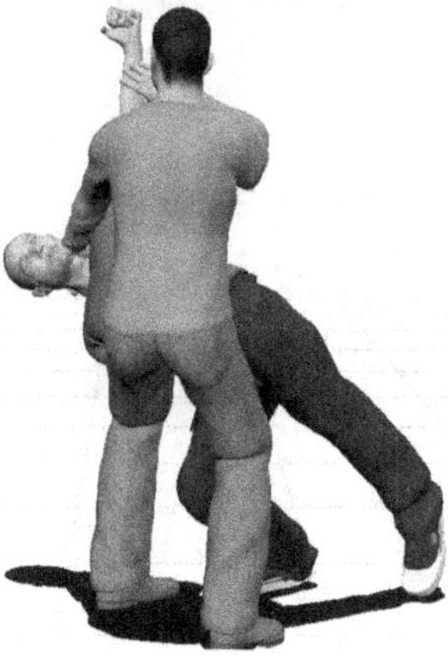

APPLICATION FIFTY-EIGHT

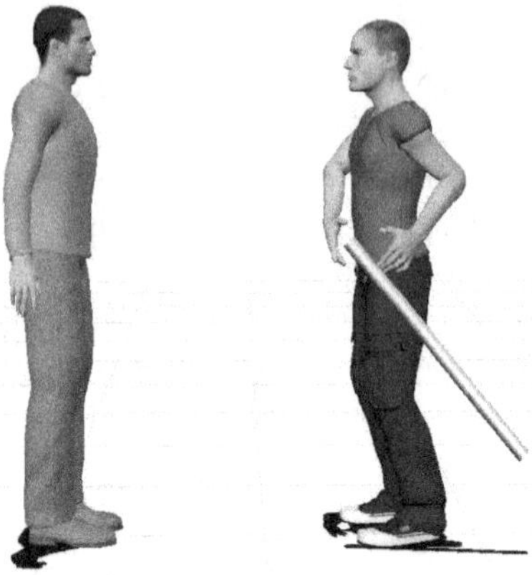

The attacker steps forward with the right foot and punches with the right hand.

The defender steps forward with the right foot and smothers the punch with his left hand as he executes a spear hand to the groin.

A spear hand?

Aside from the idea of spearing somebody in the groin with the fingers, there are all sorts of inconsistencies with this application. The block doesn't quite work with the angle of the attack.

The counter to the groin doesn't quite fit with an attack to the face.

And so on.

After much cogitation I finally realized that this technique, this move in the form, was designed to be applied when a foe reaches for a weapon.

A samurai would reach for his sword.

So how do you disarm a samurai?

You don't let him draw the sword, which might seem a stretch for some people, but is easy to understand if you have reached the ability to see what a person is going to do before he does it.

And, as long as you are stopping him from drawing his sword, you might as well draw it yourself.

Go on, get some friends and try it, you'll find that my logic is impeccable, my analysis thorough, and I'm even handsome.

And, a note, the sword is actually a butterknife I found in the particular software I use. Cool.

CONCLUSION TO THE PROMISE FIGHTS OF CHIANG NAN FIVE

As you go over the promise fights from the forms you will realize there is a progression.

The applications grow from basic to more complex (yet without sacrificing basics for 'advanced' moves).

There is a progression of chi necessary to master the techniques.

There is a progression of grab arts.

Most important, this all results in a progression of the student towards competence and mastery.

One thing no one will argue with is that martial arts are judged by what degree of competence a person has reached.

In other words, does the technique work.

Yet, we must not sacrifice art for brutality.

It is so easy to just learn to punch good; it is so easy to sacrifice your art for power, glory, or any thing else that distracts the student from the true path of the martial arts.

In the end, this competence, this mastery, if done with an eye towards technique and intention, towards polishing your technique so it takes less and less effort, will elevate the student.

Will enlighten him.

Enlightenment. An interesting word, yet bandied about with not many people understanding what it really means; with too many people visualizing mystical shards of lightening opening up their brain to give superhuman knowledge.

Yet shards of lightening may or may not occur, but irregardless of the presence of mystical experience, competence will win out.

There is the fellow who experiences lightening, sees the gods, and spends the rest of life talking about them.

Then there is the fellow who experiences no lightening, yet he becomes more and more competent.

Which would you rather have teach you? The fellow who knows, but has no competence? Or the fellow who doesn't know, but has competence pouring out of his ears.

Of course, the preference is for the teacher who has both.

But if a teacher is not present, if, indeed, you are surrounded by false teachers, then who will teach you?

The answer is self-evident: you will teach yourself.

But what people don't seem to want to recognize is that from the very first day you walk into a dojo you are teaching yourself.

Teachers lay out programs, partners suffer the bruises and breaks, but it is your experience, and you create it by persevering, persisting, suffering through no matter what distraction you may encounter.

There is no man who is not self-taught.

Make sure that you do the best you can to make sure you are taught correctly, that your real teacher is not a fool.

Chapter Eight
Chiang Nan Six

Below are the videos for form Five.

channan 6 ~ https://youtu.be/eKZBqL8PecQ	2:11
channan 6 side ~ https://youtu.be/QI2uZS4yqjM	2:09
channan 6 explained ~ https://youtu.be/Uba7BXFooB8	13:55
channan 6 app 40 ~ https://youtu.be/LLYLl2duCNQ	5:58
channan 6 app 41 ~ https://youtu.be/6lHZuDR7evM	6:38
channan 6 app 42 ~ https://youtu.be/CB7OGzGQa0E	4:16
channan 6 app 43 ~ https://youtu.be/tMniIhoF5Fs	6:00
channan 6 app 44 ~ https://youtu.be/Kt_KlY8st1Y	1:39
channan 6 app 45 ~ https://youtu.be/nk83jQZdcL4	7:33
channan 6 app 46 ~ https://youtu.be/vunGLERY-ns	1:20
	33:24

Chiang Nan Six

Channan was the original name, the working name, of this thing called Karate.

It was based on the form brought to Okinawa by a shipwrecked sailor, named Chiang Nan, or so the legend goes.

And Chiang Nan was divided into five parts, influenced by other forms, made into a template for the Imperial bodyguards, and so on.

In the Kang Duk Won I studied a variety of forms, including Sip Su, No Hai, Bot Sai, Um Be, and so on. These were all good forms. A little specific in the the types of energy they created, but very good.

The one form I learned, however, that was very similar to the Pinans was Bot Sai. The other forms were good, but I found that Bot Sai was more like a Pinan 6.

Bot Sai was a logical and appealing next step.

I tossed out the Kang Duk Won forms I had learned (Sip Su, No Hai, and Um Be) and focused on Bot Sai.

It was during Bot Sai that I started removing myself from my body, staring at my body as if from several feet behind my head, watching how fast my arms could move, how much power the stances gave.

The body, when directed by the unenlightened mind, can only move so fast. It is limited by the beliefs in the physics of the universe.

However, when enlightenment occurs the rules of physics cease to be of importance.

You know the truth of you, you know that you are a unique spirit, that your brain doesn't tell your body what to do, but rather you do.

And you, unlimited by beliefs and other such silly distractions, become capable of moving faster than a human being, trained by the physics of the universe, can.

So let's look at Bot Sai.

BOT SAI

Stand with the feet together, the right fist in the right hand.

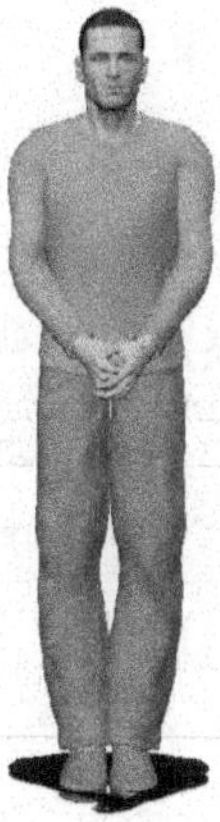

Lower the center slightly as you circle the right hand up and out through the high block position, and the left hand down through the low block position.

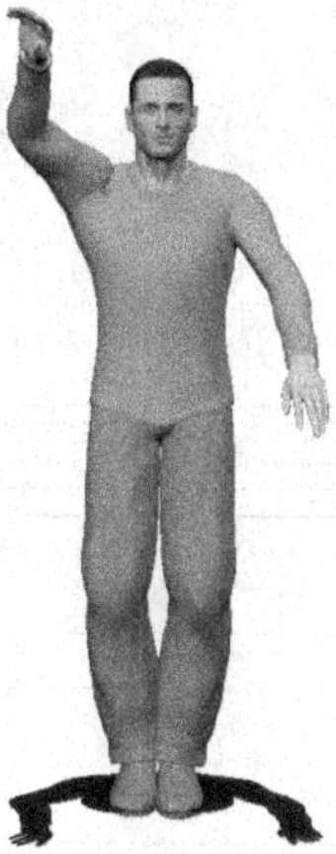

Circle the hands so that the right hand guards the groin and the left hand guards the face.

The left hand is beginning the slap/grab block.

Step forward with the right foot and bring the left foot (heel up) behind it. The feet should be in an 'X' position.

The right hand circles outward to the 'grabbing position.

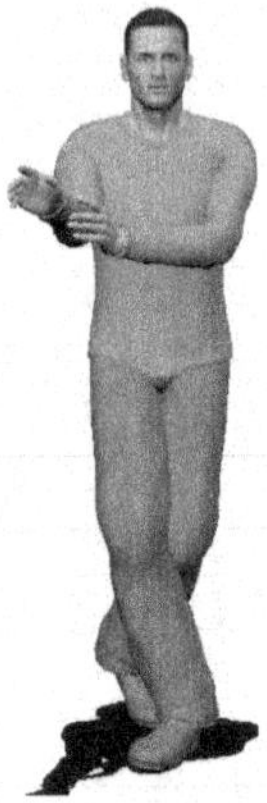

Pivot 180 degrees into an X stance as you execute a right palm block. The left foot is now in front, and the right foot is heel up behind it.

The right hand is beginning the slap/grab movement.

Side view of last image.

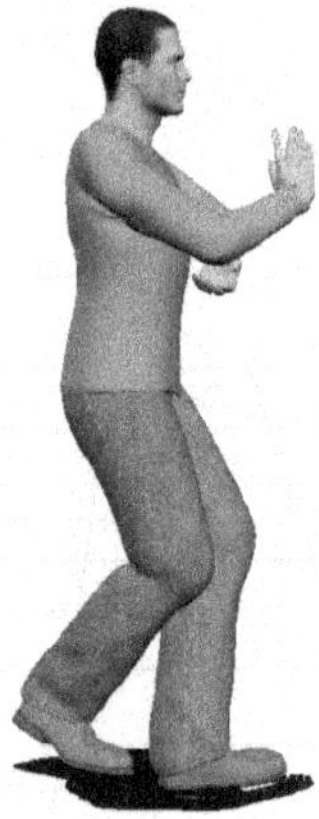

Step forward with the left foot into a font stance as you execute a left outward grabbing block.

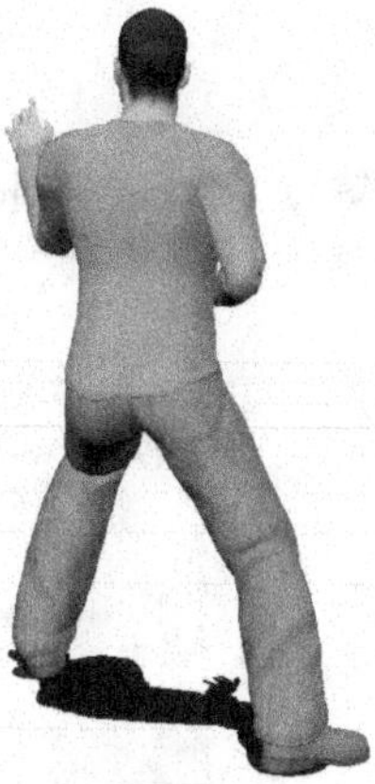

Side view of last image.

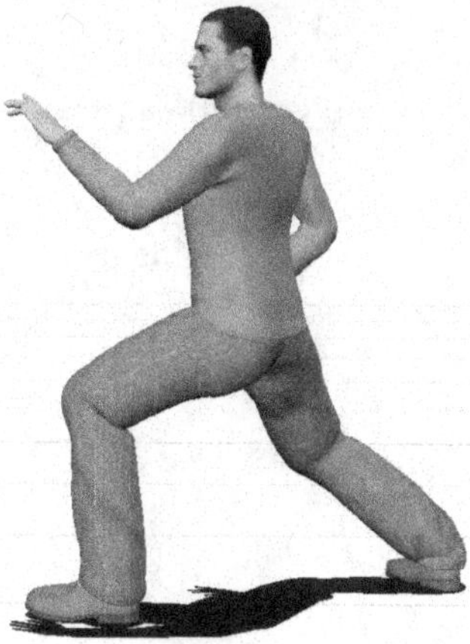

Drag the right foot slightly forward and turn it towards the left foot. The hips should turn to the right so as to support a left slap and a right grab.

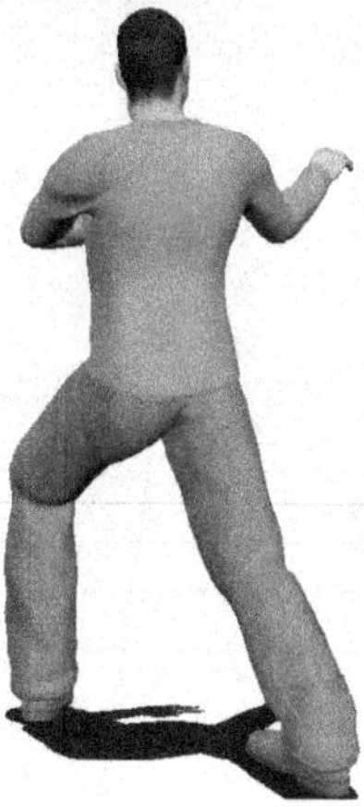

Side view of last image.

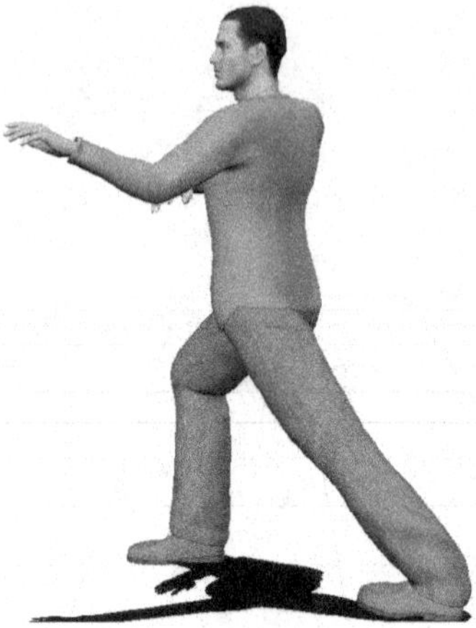

Bring the right foot behind the left foot, pivot 180 degrees into an X stance with the right foot in front.

The left hand begins the slap/grab sequence.

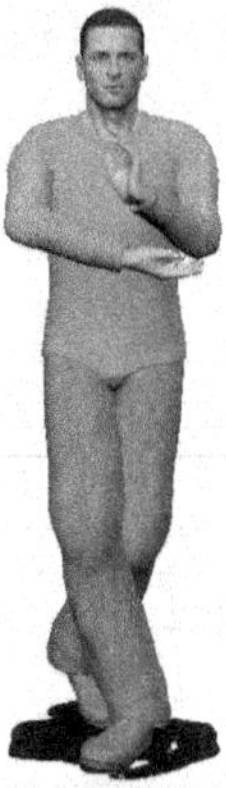

Step forward with the right foot into a front stance as you execute a right outward grabbing block.

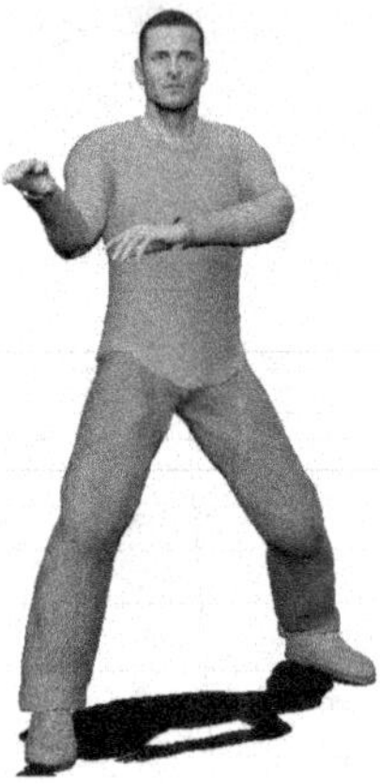

Drag the left foot slightly forward as you pivot to the left and execute a left slap and a right grab.

Bring the right foot back and turn 90 degrees to the right into a cat stance as you execute a left slap.

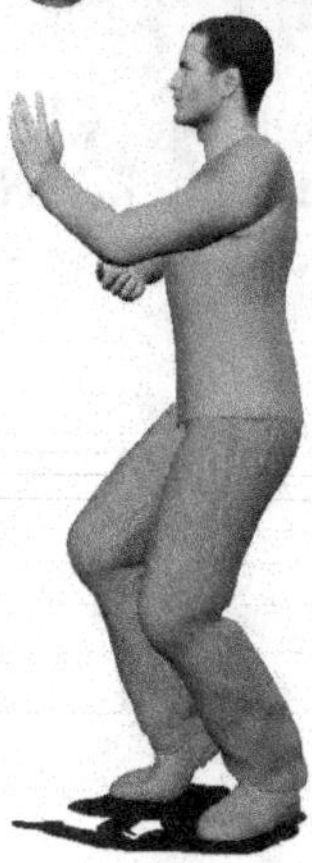

Step forward with the right foot into a front stance as you execute a right outward grabbing block.

Bring the left for slightly forward and point it at the right foot as you pivot slightly to the right and execute a right slap and a left grab.

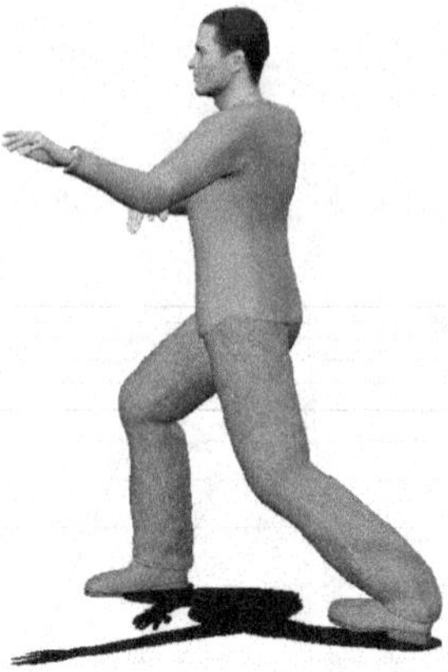

Step slightly back with the left foot (to align it with the right foot) turn into and into a horse stance as you execute a left high block.

Continue the pivot of the last move into a front stance as you execute a right spear hand to the front.

Lower the right hand and circle it across the body.

Continue the circle of the right hand to the high block position.

Continue the turn of the last move and pivot to the right into a front stance as you execute a left spear hand to the front.

Bring the left for to the right, step forward with the right foot into a back stance as you execute a right double knife hand block.

Step back and to the right with the right foot (triangle step) as you guard the face with the right hand (slap).

Step forward with the left foot into a back stance as you execute a left knife hand (grab).

Step back and to the left (triangle stepping) with the left foot as you guard the face with the left hand.

Step forward with the right foot into a back stance as you execute a right knife hand (grab).

Step back and to the right foot (triangle step) as you guard the face with the right hand.

Step forward with the left foot into a back stance as you execute a left knife hand (grab).

Step/shift forward with the left foot into a front stance as you execute double spear hands to the head.

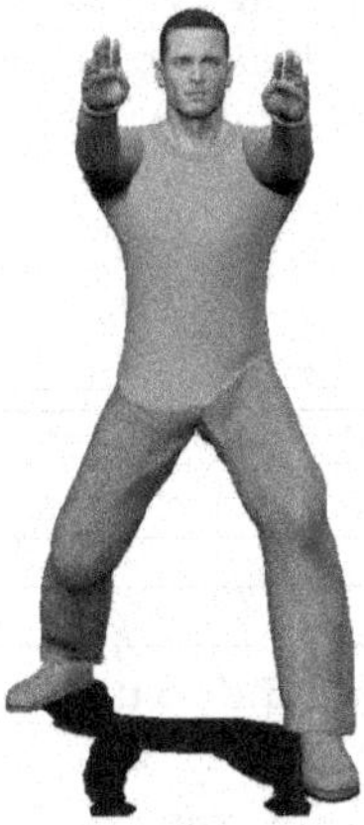

Close hands and pull as you execute a right side thrust kick to the knee.

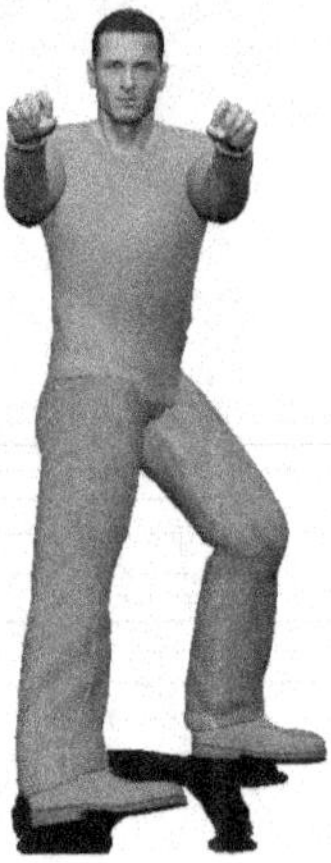

Stomp the right foot down (supercharge) as you pivot 180 degrees into a back stance as you execute a left knife hand (grab).

Step back and to the left with the left foot, step forward with the right foot into a back stance as you execute a right knife hand (grab).

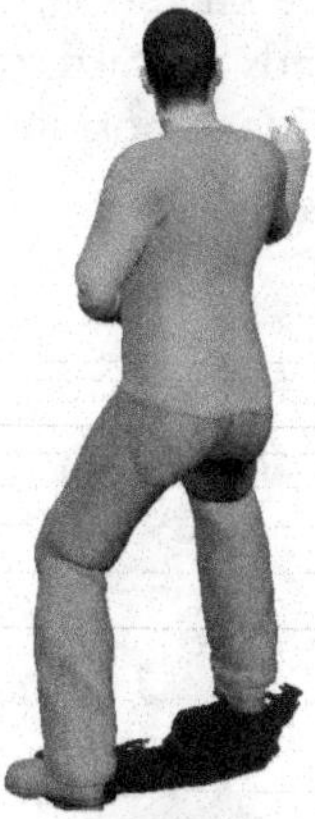

Bring the right foot back and stand up with the fists closed in front of the body.

Rear view of last image.

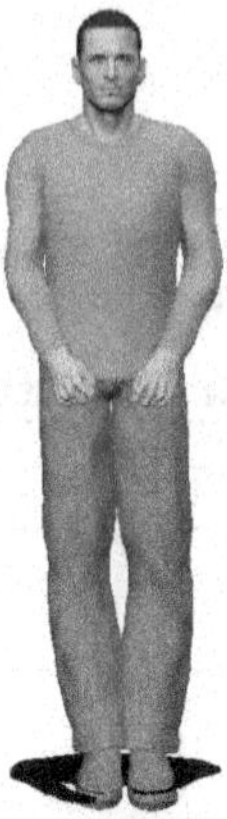

Bend the knees slightly as you bring the hands upward to the double high block position.

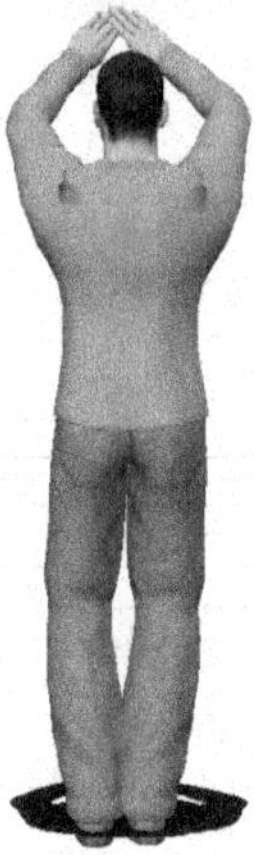

Bring the hands outward.

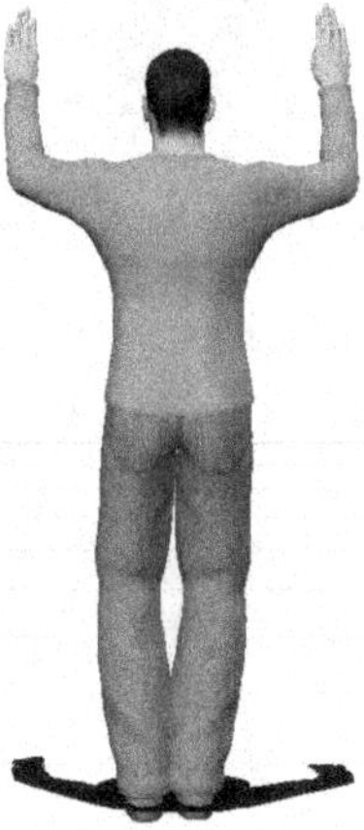

Step forward with the right foot into a back stance as you circle the hands into double palm up spear hand strikes to the front.

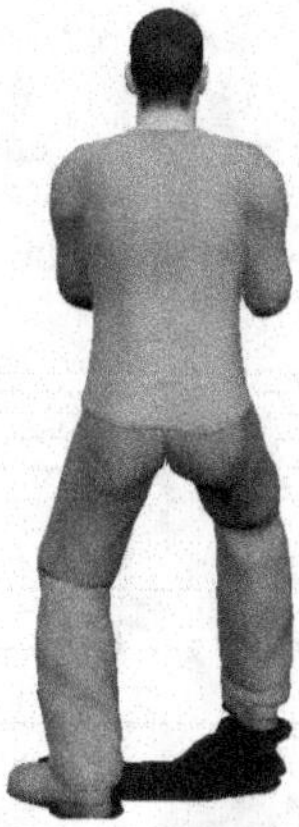

Side view of last image.

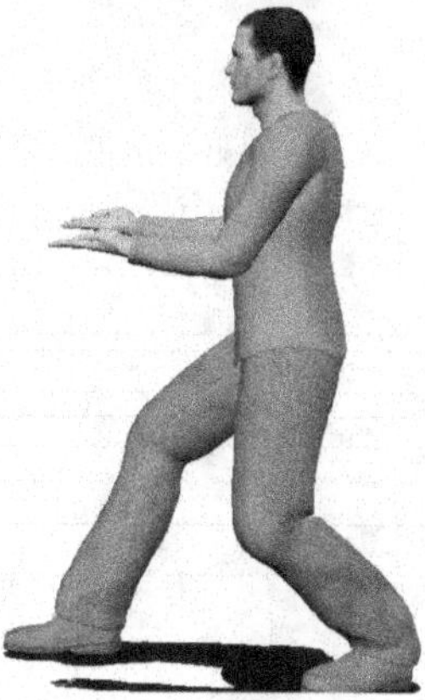

Step/shift forward with the right foot into a front stance as you execute a right spear hand to the front.

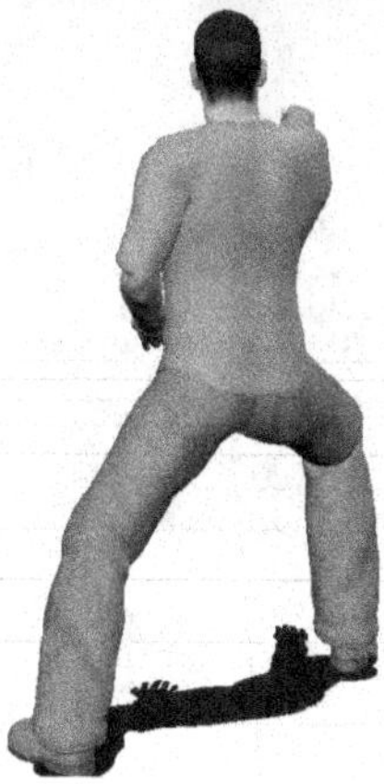

Side view of last image.

Bring the left foot next to the right and stand up straight as you pivot 90 degrees to the left and execute a left low block and a right high block.

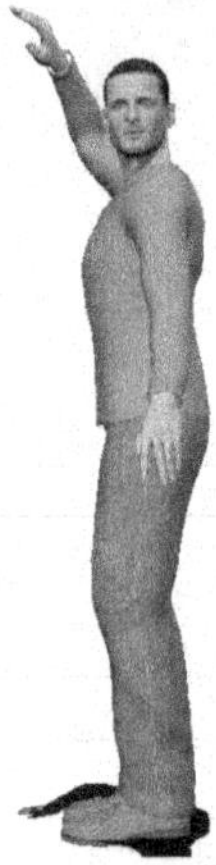

Step forward (90 degrees to the left) with the left foot into a front stance as you execute a right palm up spears hand (to the groin) and a left cross palm block.

Retract the left foot and return to the previous position.

Pivot to the left, turning the feet into an X stance as you bring the right hand forward.

Step forward into a horse stance as you circle the right hand to a low block.

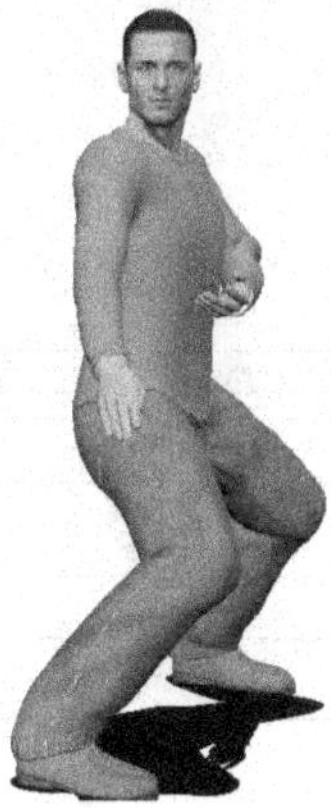

Step to the right with the right foot and pivot 180 degrees into a back stance as you swing the right flat hand.

Execute a left vertical spear hand.

Execute a right crescent kick to the left palm.

Side view of last image.

Set the right foot down in line with the left foot into a horse stance as you execute a right elbow to the left palm.

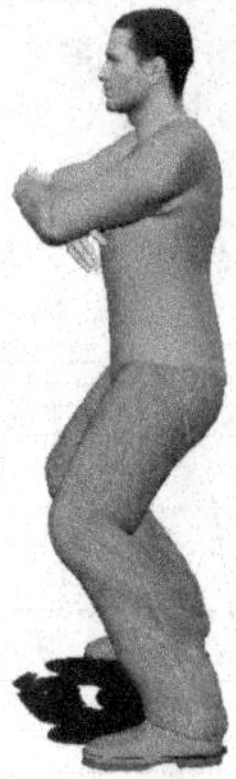

Execute a slow (dynamic tension) right low block with an open hand.

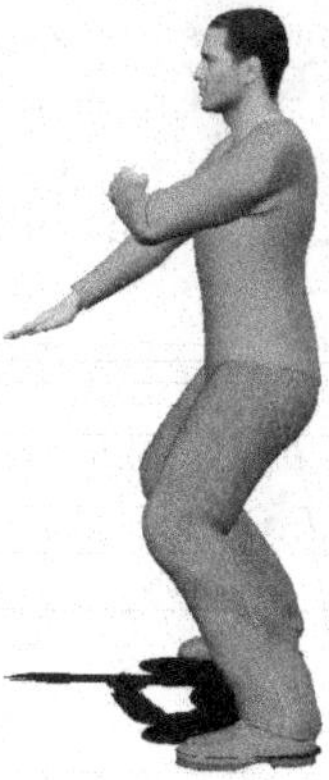

Very quickly, snap a left low block with the open hand, then a right low block with the open hand. The right hand block is pictured in the next image.

The right right hand low block with an open hand.

These two blocks should explode out of the dynamic tension low block just previous.

Pivot 90 degrees to the right as you bring the right foot next to the left and stand up. The right hand should be across the body (see next image).

Rear view of the last image.

Step forward with the right foot into a front stance as you execute an 'over/under' strike.

This is two punches, the top over the left.

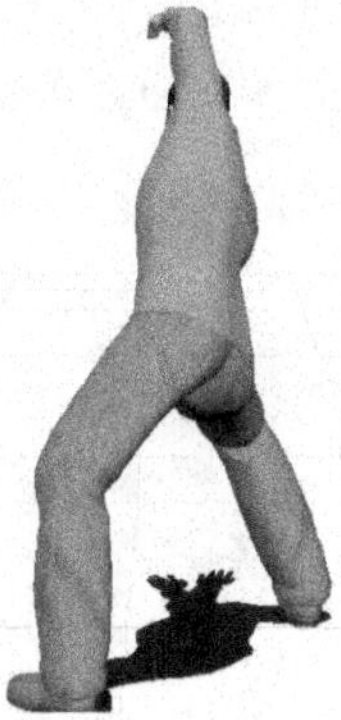

Side view of last image.

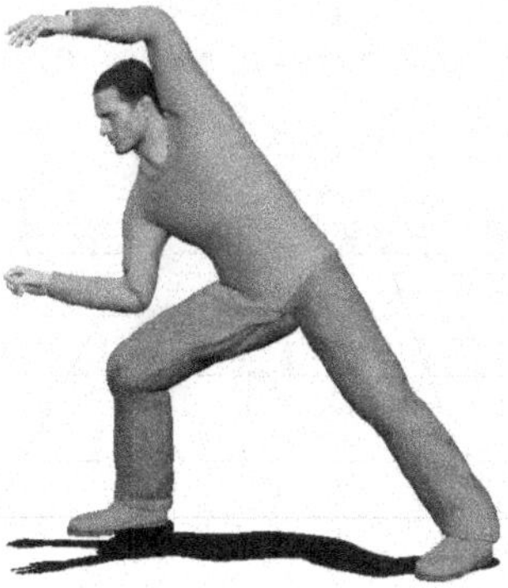

Bring the right foot back next to the left in the standing position. The left arm should be across the body as shown previously.

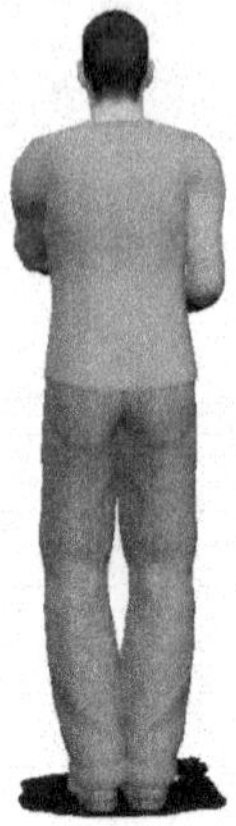

Step forward with the left foot into a front stance as you execute an 'over/under' strike.

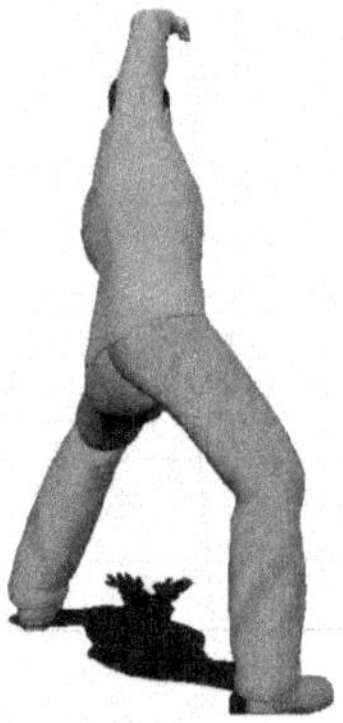

Bring the left foot back to the standing position. The right arm should be across the body as shown previously.

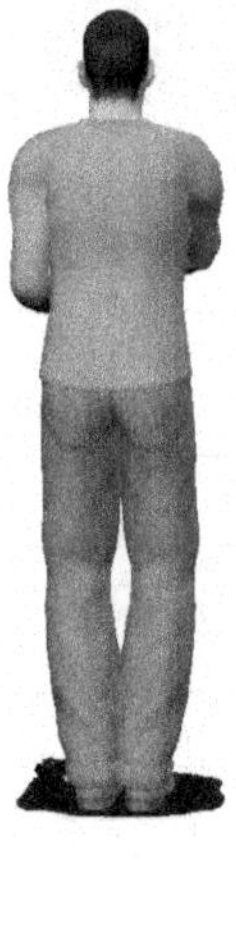

Step forward with the right foot...INTO A BACK STANCE...as you execute an 'over/under' strike.

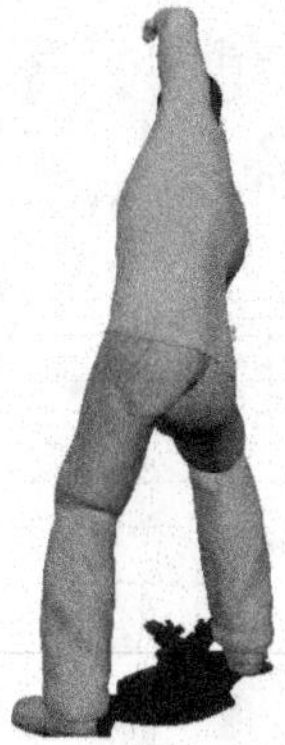

Move the left foot to the left (in line with the right foot) and pivot to the left. Sweep an inverted right low block as you pivot into a front stance.

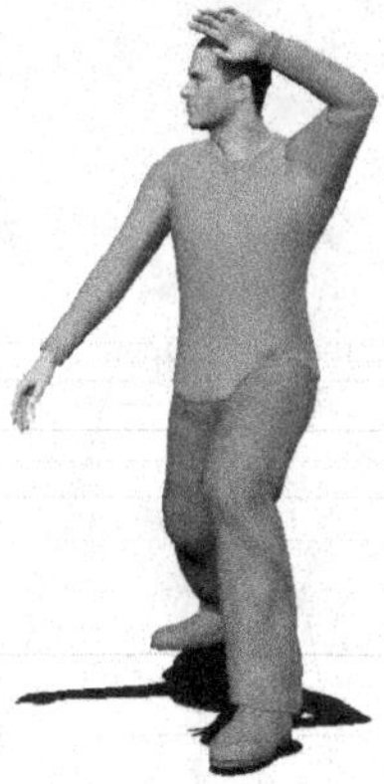

Pivot back to the right into a horse stance as you execute a right outward grabbing block.

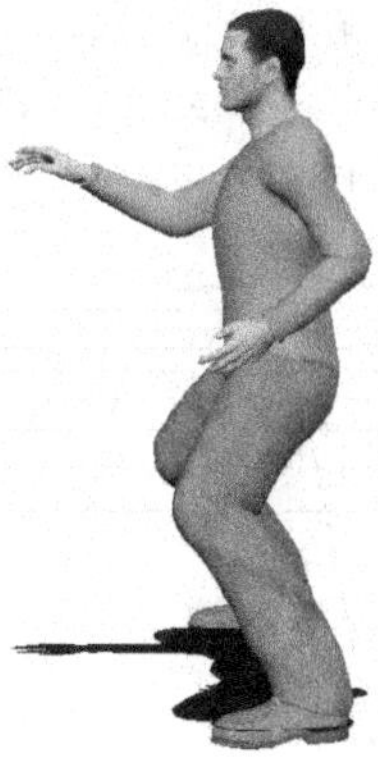

Step to the right with the right foot into a front stance as you execute a left reverse spear hand.

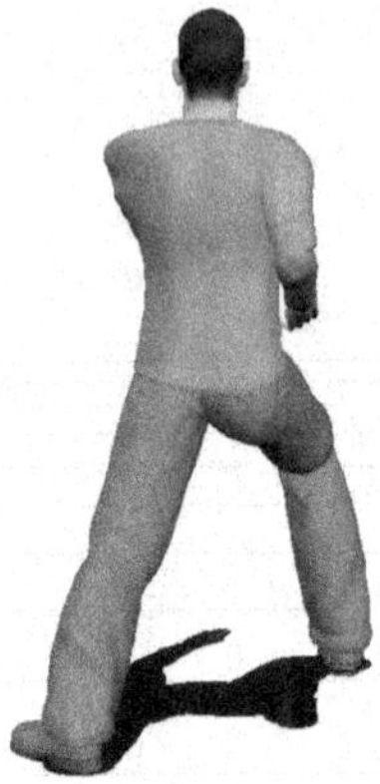

Step to the right with the left foot (in line with right foot) into a horse stance as you execute a left outward grabbing block.

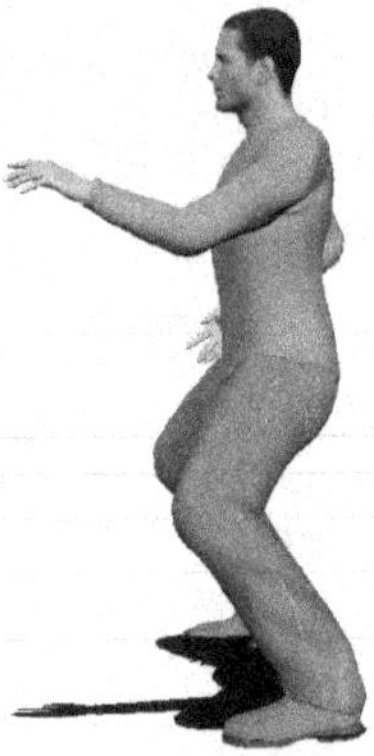

Step slightly back with the left foot and pivot to the left into a front stance as you execute a right reverse spear hand.

Step forward with the right foot into a back stance as you execute a (slap/grab) knife hand.

You can actually end the form at this point, I usually do. The following sequence, however, is the original version I learned.

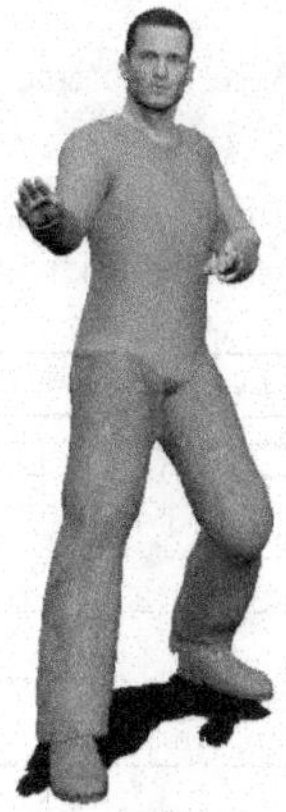

Hold your knife hand back stance and pivot on the left foot 180 degrees to the right, making a circle on the ground with the right toe. This should be done slowly, with the right toe moving smoothly and the left foot shifting imperceptibly as you turn.

Step forward with the left foot into a back stance as you execute a (slap/grab) knife hand.

Holding the posture, pivot 270 degrees to the left, the left toe describing a circle and the right foot shifting imperceptibly.

Bring the left foot back to the right foot and return to the original position from which you began the form, the right fist inside the left hand.

CHIANG NAN SIX

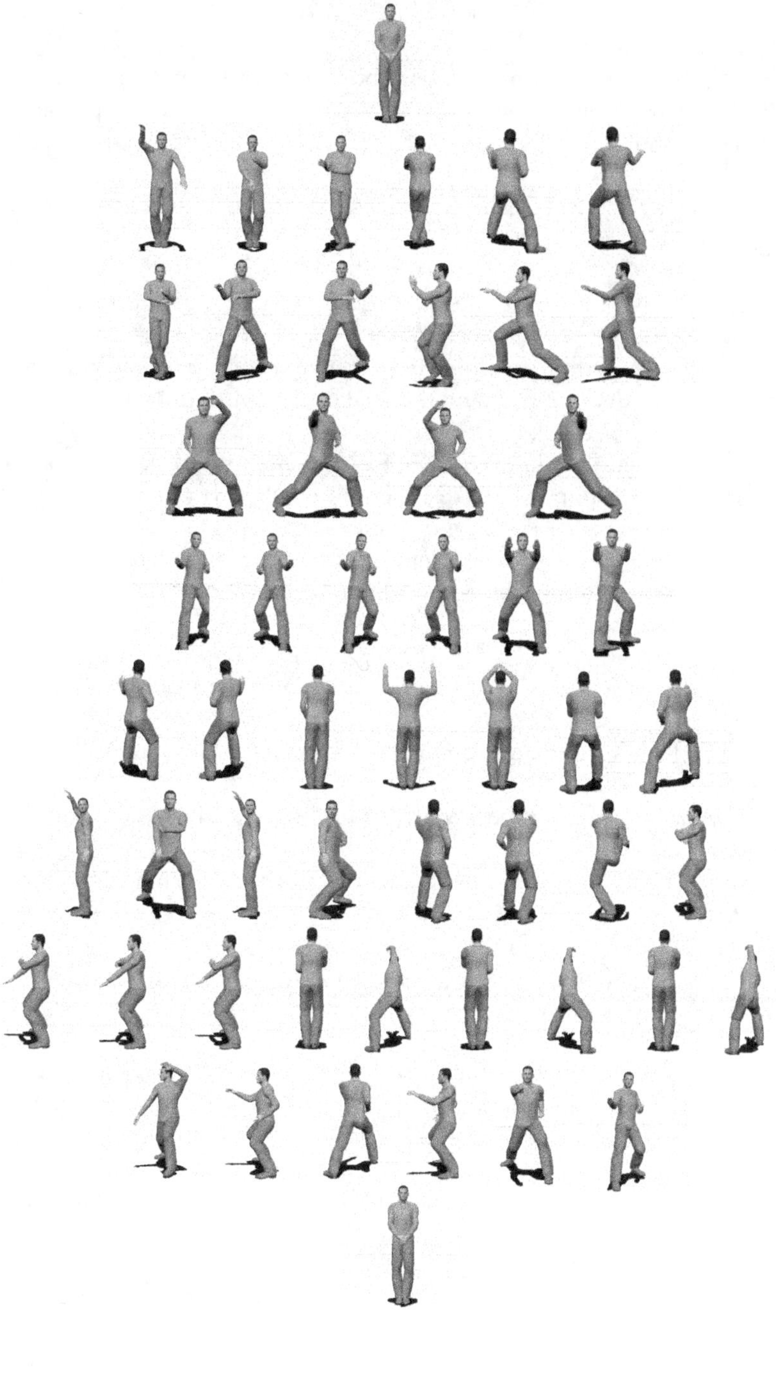

ABOUT BOT SAI

Okay, I've got some observations about this last form; this form is held up as a fairly iconic Japanese karate form, but it has a lot of problems.

Chiang Nan Six is obviously taken from Bot Sai, which is obviously 'Bassai Dai.'

It is an an advanced form, sometimes showcased as an illustration of high quality technique.

Unfortunately, they do it all wrong.

In fact, I just watched a series of videos on Bassai Dai, and I was struck by how poorly done this form was done.

The karate practitioners doing it were high quality, fantastic in body control, but they don't understand the relationship of apps to forms, nor the body physics specific to the martial arts.

Mind you, I am working with the form given to me about 1970, and with a short lineage to not Funakoshi, but to Kanken Toyama, who was one of Funakoshi's classmates, and who studied with many of the great Karate masters, including the fellow who supposedly invented the Pinan kata, taking it directly from the Chiang Nan form he was shown by the shipwrecked sailor.

So why should you consider what I say here as opposed to what you will learn in an official Japanese karate school? Why am I right and them… incorrect?

Gichin Funakoshi made a statement once that (paraphrased) 'this wasn't the karate I knew.'

So what was different between what he taught, and what he observed years later?

In the Pinans, not much, but enough to twist the meaning and nature of the forms.

The stances were stretched out to give more power.

The knife hand block was given up for a more 'strait arm' kind of knife hand.

And so on.

But one can go through the Pinans, or Heians, apply physics, and correct the form to true. There will be slight differences, but they will be recognizable as the same forms, the applications will rise in the same shape, and so on.

When you reach the advanced form, however, everything changes.

There are two points that must be made to explain this.

First, the heart and soul of Karate lies in the basics. The Pinans (Heians) explain the basics, run through the various methods of using them in self defense.

But there is only so much you can do with basics. Then you just run out of things to do.

So the advanced forms, such as Bot Sai, become odd, mystical. They offer up techniques that are advanced, require specialized situations, and are, often as not, garbage.

But remember this: there are no advanced techniques, there are only better basics.

So Bot Sai, should be about polishing the basics, reaching new depths of understanding of the basics.

But they aren't, and the form becomes altered to showcase oddities. Techniques that require amazing ability, but will never be seen in a fight. Will only be seen by a certain class of people showing off their particular athleticism.

And the physics take a drubbing.

Honestly, when I learned Bot Sai, not having any inkling of the things I tell you here, I realized that Bot Sai was for advanced athletic ability, not for fighting, and I received the most benefits from the 'mystical' feelings I got from the form.

The dynamic tension movements, the flow of power through certain sequences, and so on.

Except for one, and only one, technique.

Which made me blink, for the form was full of techniques, but there as only one technique that advanced me (and seriously, to be truthful) in the martial arts.

That technique was in the first three movements after the initial stomping outward blocking movement, the inward/outward blocking sequences.

This was the first time I had been required to block three punches (strikes) in a row.

During the Pinans, and even in the forms after the Pinans and before Bot Sai, I first learned the single defense, then blocking two strikes, but never three.

And, in that three strike self defense (which I will show you in the section on Promise Fights), there was a movement of the body that was impossible.

The attacker has but a short strike to your body.

You have to twist and loop your fist, with the whole body behind it, moving twice as far as the attack, to make it work.

Shockingly (to me), I was able to make it work.

But in making it work I had to move beyond muscle and remove myself from my body.

As I learned to do the technique I, the spiritual awareness, the I am that I am, simply moved backwards from my head, out of my body, and I watched my hands and body move faster and with more purity than I had ever imagined possible.

Doing that technique became the most peaceful moment in my life. The fast and utterly frantic action resolved into me disassociating myself from the body, operating it from outside the body, and achieving an understanding of my true self that simply does not exist in western society.

Here was all the mystical zen I would ever need.

One pure technique that made me move faster than I could, and so enlightened me.

Now, that all said, let's get back to Bot Sai and take it apart so you can understand what was done to it, and how it can be resurrected to, if not it's original form, something that will do for you what it did for me.

Let's do this piece by piece, and without thinking about applications.

Let's just consider the physics now, and then look at it all again in the applications.

BOT SAI EXPLAINED

The first move of Bot Sai is often done wrong. Consider the move shown below.

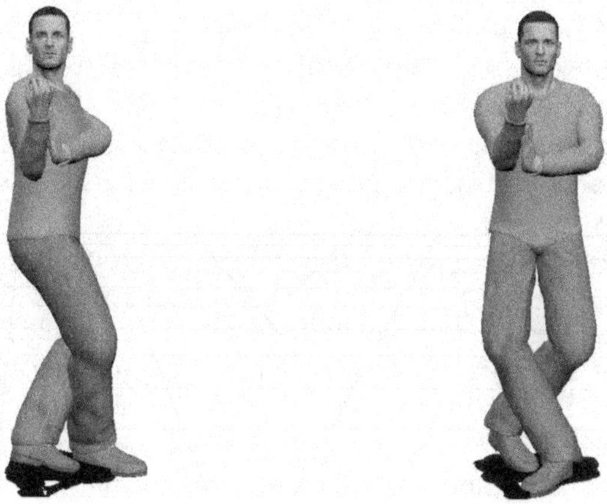

In the figure on the left, which you will see here and there, the karate has his hips turned to the side.

In the figure on the right the hips are to the front, what I refer to as 'square.'

When you do this move, as you will see when we extract the Promise Fight, you are leaping to the front. But if you turn your hips to the side then you are going in two directions at once. You are splitting your intention, and thus robbing your technique of 50% of the power. At minimum.

This is easy to prove, simply push on the block. Test the body and you will quickly see that when the body is turned sideways the energy doesn't go through the body to the ground, rather body gives way.

When the body is square then the rear hand can work to augment the bock and help it stay in place.

This technique is designed to close distance. It is better as a jamming block, but can be used as an outright strike.

One doesn't usually augment a strike, however, as that has the potential of detracting from the blocking abilities of the rear hand. As one moves into advanced forms, however, this can be explored.

Another item to be noted is that in this Promise Fight i will be striking with the closed fist. This demands a certain discussion of when I close my fists, and when not.

I have beginners close their fists, this to protect their fingers.

In the form I show open hands, but this can obviously be tailored for the technique or student.

As a student becomes more competent I have this advice: strike with the number of fingers you can do a push up with.

When you strike somebody you are, in essence, supporting (overwhelming) his weight.

Thus, if you weight 200 pounds, you can strike with a fist if you can do a push up on your fist, because that shows your fist can support the impact of 200 pounds.

If you can do a push up on your fingers you can strike with your fingers.

I reached a certain point in my training where I could do push ups on the two fingers of my two hands. This means I could strike people with two fingers.

But, to be honest, I don't strike with the fingers so much as place them on the attacker's body and insert them.

Play with the next application, see when you can use open hands for blocks, and when you have to close the fists.

So let me show you the Promise Fight that I use this move for.

APPLICATION FIFTY-NINE

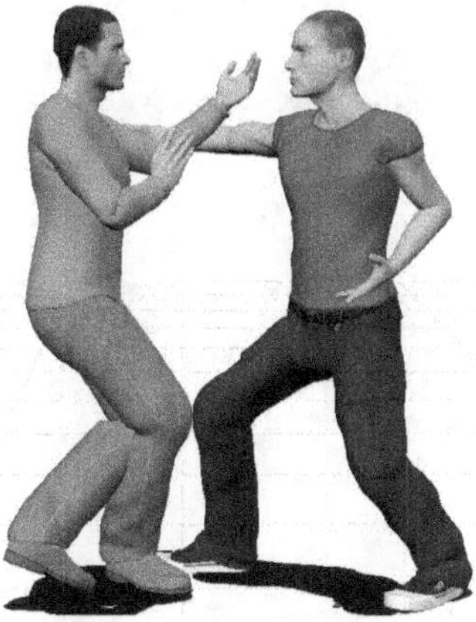

The attacker steps forward with the right foot and punches with the right hand.

The defender moves forward into an X stance with an augmented left outward block.

There should be a light stamp of the front foot to 'supercharge' the technique.

The defender lifts his right foot slightly.

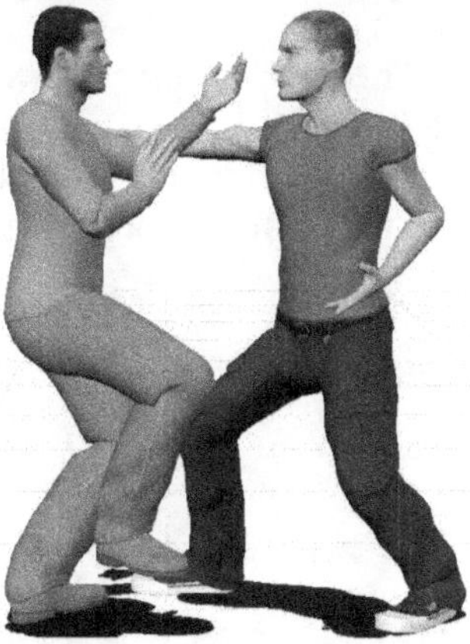

The defender stomps (gently) the right foot, supercharging his right fist as he strikes the attacker.

This technique requires two 'superchargings,' it is designed to summon immense power while too close in too use hip rotation or thrust.

Thus, the stomp increases gravity and feeds power to the strike.

APPLICATION SIXTY

The attacker steps forward with the right foot and punches with the right hand.

The defender steps back with the left foot into a front stance as he executes a left palm block. The hips should be 'square' to the front.

The attacker punches with the left hand.

The defender pivots slightly to the left as he executes a right inward block.

The attacker punches with the right hand.

The defender twists his stance to the right and circles the left hand under to execute a left outward block.

The defender pushes forward, shuffling his whole weight into a left punch.

This last move is the one that made me pop out of my head. The attacker has a straight line foot to punch, I have to twist my body (a lot of mass) and move the hand through a couple of feet of arc.

The interesting thing about this technique is that when you finally strike you are wound up, the twisting back and forth has squeezed the body downward, and it is ready to come unsprung. Whole lot of power here.

At this point in your training you should be holding your ground. Power is the ability to hold your position, and this technique really ups the ante; it really makes you stay right in the face of the storm.

And, for those who didn't get it, here is that little gem of physics specific to the martial arts, and to the entire universe:

Power is your ability to hold your position.

A NOTE ON THE KNIFE HAND

This is a good place to insert this little note.

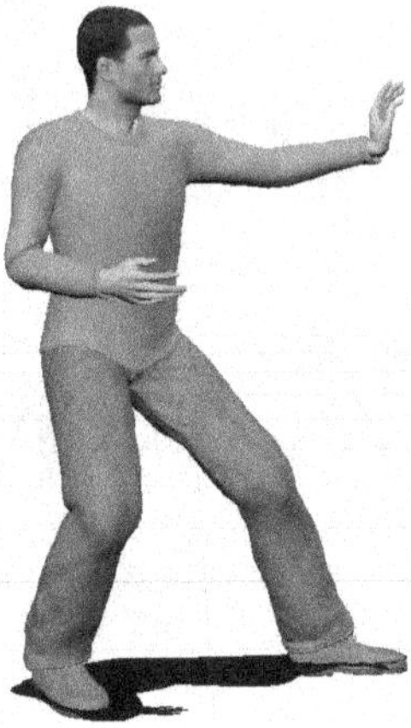

The figure on the left is doing the knife hand block as many in the Japanese systems do it, with the arm extended almost like a 'straight arm' block.

The figure on the right is the way we did this block 50 years ago, fresh out of Korea and Okinawa.

The reason for this change?

I don't know.

I do know that if you over extend your arm you are giving your opponent a lever to grab.

And I know that if you understand the slap/grab concept then you can use the block as a simple chopping tool, or you can use it as it is used in the next application.

APPLICATION SIXTY-ONE

The attacker steps forward with the right foot and punches with the right hand.

The defender steps to the left into a horse stance as he circles the right hand in an outward grabbing block.

This is a catching and guiding motion!

The defender continues the direction of his right arm and turns his body to the right into a front stance. This gives his left punch more distance, and utilizes the entire mass of the twisting hips. As he twists he pulls, with his entire body weight, the attacker's wrist.

The downward punch can be a pubic punch, punching down at the waist (where the upper leg connects and bends) so that the attacker falls back and down.

Many people do a chop at this part of the form. If you examine the physics you will find that it is not particularly strong, though the horse stance makes it feel strong.

Thus, I translated the chop into a high block, and made the whole move fluid, teaching a certain flow of technique.

A NOTE ON DYNAMIC TENSION

There are a couple of moves in this form, in most of the advanced forms, which I note as requiring 'dynamic tension.' Considering the last move, now is probably a good time to discuss dynamic tension.

The original dynamic tension, here in the states, referred to a type of body building. One presses one palm against the other and pushes it. The palm being pushed resists and moves but slowly. The palm pushing uses muscles to make the push.

This method was advertised in comic books quite a bit, I believe the 'bully kicks sand in the face' were the specific ads, though I could be mistaken.

In the martial arts one moves slowly, and the tension is the set of muscles on one side of a limb against the muscles on the other side of a limb.

This particular move feels powerful, looks powerful, and does create power.

But the power is not just muscular, it is energetical.

Unfortunately, you often see karate doing a move slowly, significantly, and not really delving into the power potential.

This is because, usually, they are applying dynamic tension to the wrong move. Or they are making the form look good, and not really exerting themselves.

The last move is should be done with dynamic tension, the turn of the hips requiring massive amounts of power pushed through the legs, the arm moved through space as if it is moving a thousand pounds.

So that is what dynamic tension is, and what you should be doing when I mention it in conjunction with a particular move.

A NOTE ON A KICK

I have seen many ways of messing up this particular move. It is the kick done at the end of four knife hand blocks.

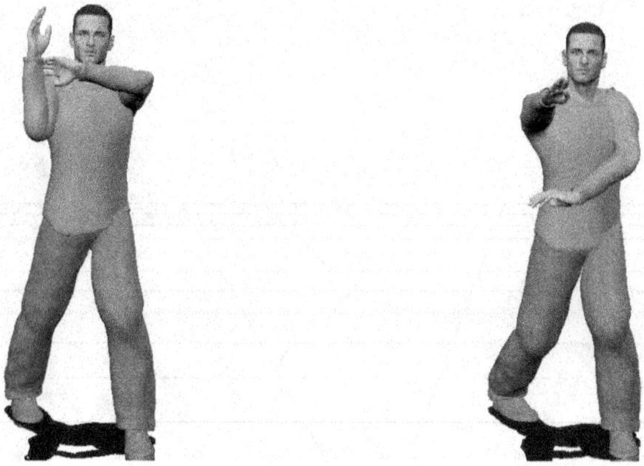

The figure on the left puts his hands up in some kind of block. I have seen this several ways, so I just draw this generic sort of 'what if' block.

The way we originally did this form was as the figure on the right does it, with a spear hand and a smoother block. The spear hand, interestingly enough, was supposed to be a split finger strike specifically to the eyes. I just use a spear.

The problem here is that if you are close enough to block you are probably too close to kick.

If you lean in to spear the eyes the attacker will jerk backwards, and now you might be far enough away to launch a kick, especially if the attacker is larger than you.

The guy who tries to beat you up will probably be taller than you. That is just the cowardly nature of bullies; they don't want to pick on somebody who is bigger than them.

And, you could use the supercharge kick in a replacement style, switching the feet and stomping (supercharging) as you kick.

APPLICATION SIXTY-TWO

The attacker steps forward with his right foot and punches with his right hand.

The defender steps forward and to the left into a front stance as he executes a left smother block and a right spear to the eyes.

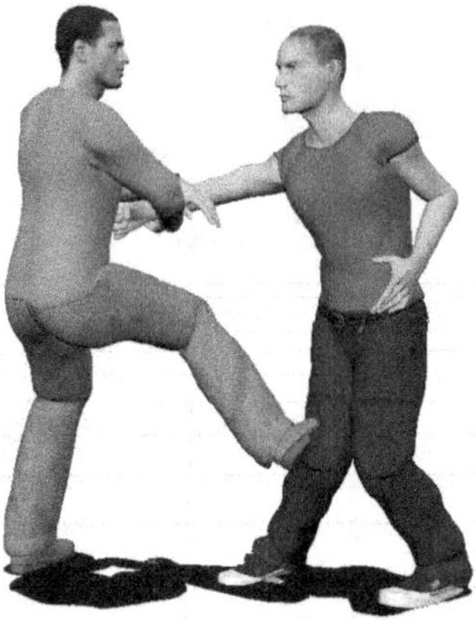

The defender scoops the right arm under the attacker's arm, catching and pulling. At the same time he hops (as he needs to to adjust for distance) and drives a right side kick through the attacker's knee.

You may notice that the promise fights are taking place at closer distances.

It is a beginner that needs distance, and the longer time that goes with distance, to learn to observe opponents and judge them accordingly.

The advanced student doesn't need reaction time, he has learned how to judge when and how an opponent is going to move before he moves, and his distances are as if the fight is taking place 'inside a phone booth.'

APPLICATION SIXTY-THREE

The attacker steps forward with the right foot and punches to the face with the right hand.

The defender steps back with the left foot into a back stance as he raises double high blocks.

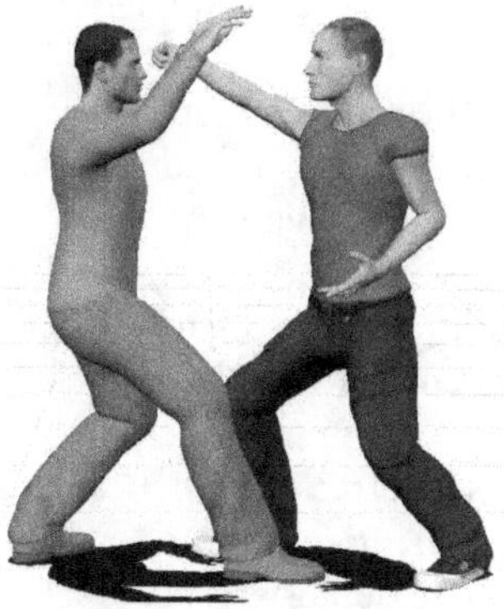

The defender circles his hands to execute double uppercuts to the mid-section.

The defender steps forward with the right foot into a front stance and punches with the right hand.

The uppercuts should lodge under the floating ribs, breaking the ribs while pushing the attacker back.

The attacker should be pushed back by the uppercuts, necessitating the drive forward.

The defender can punch with either hand on the last move, depending on the distance he has to cover.

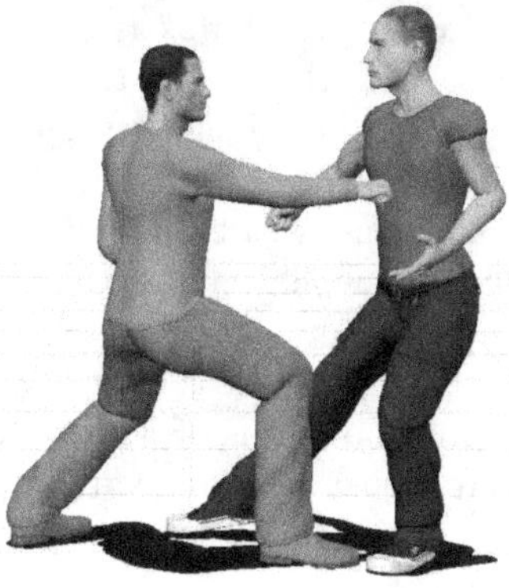

APPLICATION SIXTY-FOUR

The attacker steps forward with the right foot and punches with the right hand.

The defender steps back with the left foot into a back stance as he executes a right low block.

The attacker punches with the left hand.

The defender pulls the right foot slightly back and twists to the right as he executes a left low block.

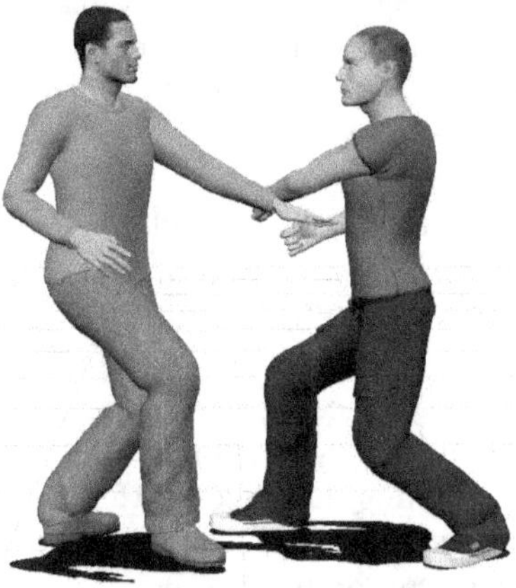

The defender steps forward with the left foot into a front stance, pushing the attacker's right knee with his left knee to break the balance, and pushing on the attacker's left arm to throw him back.

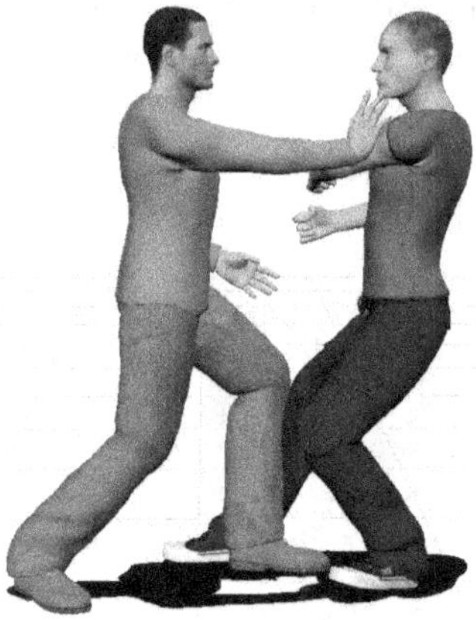

We used to do this as a defense for kicks, and by this time the student should have strong enough blocks to block kicks. But if you do this twist block for punches you will learn how to twist your body faster than punches. Also, there is control and manipulation that is of a higher level than just smashing with a fist. Although, smile, you can certainly do that, to.

CONCLUSION TO THE PROMISE FIGHTS OF CHIANG NAN

One begins by learning the basic blocks, which is handy for learning relaxing, grounding, breathing, body alignment, and so on. Learning the basic tools of karate.

As one progresses the blocks become more useful, usable in actual freestyle, and definitely in actual combat.

As one achieve expertise they should translate into softer techniques.

Learn how to insert a single finger or two, and instead of bashing, pressing so that an opponent is thrust away easily and with much verve

Learn how to slide a block, guide a block, manipulate the incoming force away with little force, and with much flow.

Learn how to take a fellow down not by violent turns of the hips and slamming of the bodies, but by adjusting a stance, turning a knee.

In the end, you will never have to fight.

For I tell you this: you learn to fight not to fight, but so that you never have to fight. So that people will look at you and instinctively trust you, feel your calmness pervading the very air, understand that you are not a violence bringer, but a peacemaker, and that on the deepest levels of the human spirit.

Once you have mastered the art, the art has mastered you, and you will always be protected, and you will always be that person who society relies on for sanity in times of crisis, and strength in times of peace.

CONCLUSION TO THIS BOOK

I began this book with the lofty idea of translating karate into Tai Chi.

Did I succeed?

I think so, though with some caveat.

It is not Tai Chi, nor is it meant to be Tai Chi. It is meant to offer a different way of doing Karate, of adjusting karate techniques towards more efficiency, and the eventual outcome of less energy being required.

And, of course, another way of using Tai Chi to rehab the body, strengthen, and so on.

Borrowing strengths from one art to bolster up another.

On the path of this book I discovered that I was delving deeper into technique than I had ever done.

Not into more twisty and glorious 'advanced' techniques that only an Olympic contortionist who cross trains in Parcour can do, but a softer, more efficient, less energy method of application.

And I found myself wondering if I was tapping into the original concepts of the founders of Karate, and of the martial arts.

Was I delving into the 'Chiang Nan' form that was originally brought to Okinawa by some shipwrecked sailor? (As the legend goes.)

On certain levels I thought so.

I think I did make the same moves, be it in altered fashion, that that shipwrecked sailor showed to Ankoh Itosu.

Of course, there will probably be much argument concerning this. My arrogance, of course, that I could actually consider myself in such fashion, and…so on.

But one does not succeed in the martial arts, one does not reach the level of the true martial artist, by being a simple copycat, by only doing what has been done before.

One reaches the true art by stepping outside the box, by asking questions, tough questions, and then forcing his eyes to stay open when the answers present themselves.

And the answers will present themselves to the person who studies diligently, who does the forms, and is willing to step forth.

Do the forms until the forms do you.

Let your spirit step forth.

Shine, and the world be damned, and you will have the true art.

Finally, did I tap into the original bunker of the Okinawan bodyguards?

On this I feel much certainty.

I studied an art removed from the founders by only four or five generations.

I learned this art in the late sixties, and, though I have gone in many ways, walked down many paths, studied many other arts, I have kept this art true, the way it was shown to me.

And even though I have made small changes in this book, you can find my original book on Kang Duk Won if you wish to find exactly what I was taught, the exact form of the original Kang Duk Won.

That said, I think I have done my very best with this tool I have been given, this original Karate, this martial art with so many facets.

In closing,I give you my thanks.

I bow to you, the generations to come.

I hope that I have set aa good example, or, at least, if my example is bad, it can be learned from.

Have a great work out!

Al Case

MORE

For those students who wish to understand more concerning how Nine Square Diagram Boxing evolved was designed and put together, go to:

MonsterMartialArts.com

And if you wish to simply explore my other writings,, including novels, poetry, etc., go to:

AlCaseBooks.com

On the following pages you will find a sampling of martial arts books.

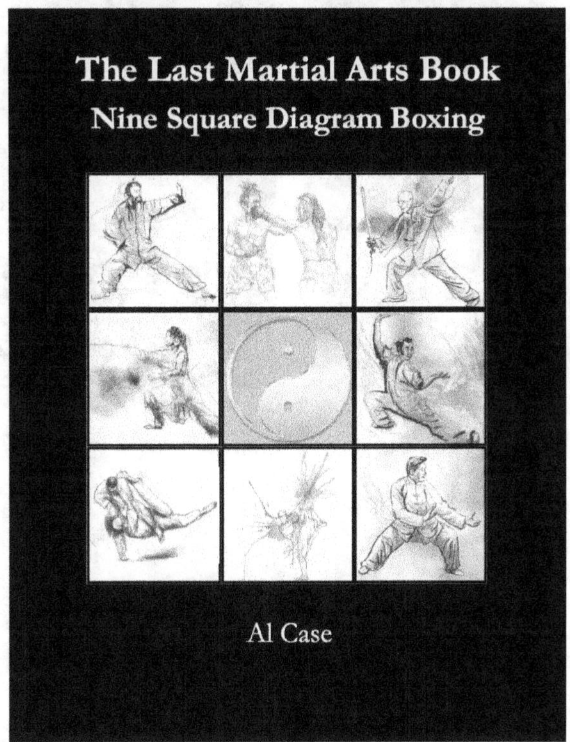

THE BOOK OF MATRIXING

Matrixing is the most important development of the martial arts in history.
This volume holds three books written by the 'inventor' of Matrixing, Al Case.

These three books are NOT books of technique and form, but are directly concerned with the logic and theory of matrixing.
The books are:

Martial Arts 101: Fixing the Martial Arts The Science of Matrixing in the Martial Arts Binary Matrixing in the Martial Arts

This is not a book of forms/ techniques.

Available on the Internet.

THE BOOK OF NEUTRONICS

Behind the Martial Arts there is a philosophy, it is called Neutronics. This book, The Book of Neutronics,' is the culmination of over 50 years studying the martial arts, all martial arts. It is a compilation of five previously published books: The Neuronic Viewpoint, Prologue, The 24 Principles, Neutronics, Outside the Tube. It is recommended that the reader be a martial artist, or study martial arts while reading this book. One who reads without doing is a 'paper tiger,' and that is to be avoided.

This is not a book of forms/ techniques.

Available on the Internet.